Gathering Ground

Gathering Ground

A READER
Celebrating Cave Canem's
First Decade

Toi Derricotte and Cornelius Eady, Editors
Camille T. Dungy, Assistant Editor

Introduction by Elizabeth Alexander,
Harryette Mullen, and the Editors

The University of Michigan Press
Ann Arbor

Copyright © by the University of Michigan 2006
All rights reserved
Published in the United States of America by
The University of Michigan Press
Manufactured in the United States of America
⊗ Printed on acid-free paper

2009   2008   2007   2006   4   3   2   1

A CIP catalog record for this book is available from the British Library.

Library of Congress Cataloging-in-Publication Data applied for.

ISBN 0-472-09924-8 (cloth)
ISBN 0-472-06924-1 (paper)

Contents

Preface

Cave Canem is a nonprofit organization for African American poets founded in 1996 by Toi Derricotte and Cornelius Eady. Each summer fifty-two poets (about seventeen new poets a year, with the remainder returning for their second or third summers) take part in a one-week workshop/retreat. Over the past ten years over two hundred poets have gone through Cave Canem's summer program. Since they return to the workshop/retreat for three years during a five-year period, Cave Canem poets have built a network of connections and support that lasts well beyond the workshop week in June. Cave Canem Fellows and faculty have won a significant number of prizes and awards, including several NEA fellowships, several Guggenheim awards, the Whiting Award, the National Poetry Series, the Dorset Prize, a Bush Fellowship, and nominations for the National Book Award and the National Book Critics Circle Award. Cave Canem poets cover a range of styles (formal, experimental, and performance, to name a few broad groups) and often move between boundaries, creating new and exciting modes for their poems. The poems collected in this anthology reflect these accomplishments and the range of styles, modes, and forms used by Cave Canem poets.

Gathering Ground: A Reader Celebrating Cave Canem's First Decade includes sonnets, a bop (a new form created by a Cave Canem faculty member), blues, sestinas, several poems in various nonce forms, prose poems, centos, and a wide variety of poems in free verse. The poems collected here provide a window to the wide range of poets (emerging and established) present in today's African American poetry community who also are making (or have made) names for themselves beyond the black community.

—Camille Dungy

Introduction

Cornelius Eady

There are many roads that lead to what we now know as the Cave Canem workshop. Perhaps mine partly begins here, in December 1990, talking to Charles Rowell for an unpublished interview for *Callaloo:*

ROWELL: Well, we could ask, Is it worth it all? There are those young black writers who could be crushed by such a program and such hostile professors. Should we be going about trying to construct certain alternatives in African American communities? I can't think that white communities, as collectives, would be seriously interested in identifying, encouraging, nurturing, and developing young African American writers.

EADY: Well . . . I really wish in my heart of hearts, I wish there were some way we could set up MFA programs just for black writers. I mean, I know that sounds kind of extreme, but I really think that there are a lot of writers out there who are going to go into those other programs. Like my own experience in an MFA program . . . I didn't see myself, my life, reflected in any of the writers that got discussed or were assigned. We simply didn't exist. And after a while I had to start thinking, "Well, wait . . . what does that mean about how they perceive me as a student? I don't exist on their level. I'm not there. They don't teach me. They don't teach me because they don't know me." I was there for two years, and that was my experience . . . I am being told to write from my life, but yet on the other hand they don't understand why I'm talking about this or why I'm bringing this in . . . So what if there was a summer workshop for just minority writers? They could come in and talk about literature but also know one thing they would not have to worry about when they walked into the workshop is . . . being the only black person, or the only Latino, or . . . It would be nice if there were ways that we could simply let these young writers know that isn't really an issue in terms of developing themselves as writers. That in fact it could be looked on as a plus. And don't get me wrong. I'm not saying that I want to forgive every mistake that they make as writers, or that we should encourage bad writing. I'm not encouraging that at all, but I do notice that there is this other criterion that sometimes enters into the discussion of what a poem is, or what makes a poem good or not good in a workshop . . . It would be nice if sometimes, occasionally, you could have a situation where a black writer didn't have to worry about that, if you talked about the *poem* as opposed to "oh you're a black person talking about being a black person, and I'm a white person, and that makes me a little nervous, and I don't know if I want to talk about that." . . . For a black writer, there is always a possibility that you are going to have to deal with it.

I could tell you that this part of our conversation was regarding the low level of minority representation in MFA writing programs; or that I'd had a similar conversation a few months earlier with Herman Beavers (who ironically would be in the first group of Cave Canem fellows) at the bar at B. Smith; or that another part of my reply came from a problem that Cathy McKinley, one of two African American students in the poetry workshop I taught at Sarah Lawrence College, had trying to convince the others in the workshop that a poem she had written about her grandmother was indeed a poem—how it was less about the draft's merits, an attempt at praise-song, than the impatient tone in the room, the realization that this discussion wasn't just about poetry, and the look on her face that said she was *suddenly on her own*, a feeling I knew and had swallowed (and was swallowing with her) but couldn't yet fully articulate or defend myself or her against.

All of that was informing my response to Charles, but what haunts me most in rereading my words, fifteen years later, is the intense longing inside them: *Wouldn't it be great to build a space where you didn't have to apologize? Where you didn't have to explain?*

I was talking tough, but I was pining for a home. So was Charles, so was Herman, so was Cathy. And most important, though we had yet to meet, so was Toi.

How best to describe Cave Canem? We have been at this for ten years now, and quite frankly, it's still tough to get a handle on it. On the surface, our core program is still a workshop/retreat, like all the few dozen or so that take place every summer across the country. People show up; workshops are held; drafts are picked at; ideas and numbers are exchanged.

Plus, we're certainly not the only workshop that has dealt with poets of color. Years before Cave Canem began, Tom Ellis and Sharon Strange and others from the Dark Room Collective invited me to come and read for them at their space in Cambridge, Massachusetts. It was like being part of a Sunday revival meeting. A crowd showed up (I couldn't tell who actually lived there and who didn't), some furniture got moved, some chairs unfolded, and Pow! Their living room turned into a salon. I guess I refer to the energy of a revival because that's how they all seemed to take it: with a serious joy and pride in their belief in being black *and* being wordy, which totally disarmed me. Perhaps that was the first time I saw that sort of idea acted on.

And though June Jordan's tenure as director of the Poetry Center at the State University of New York at Stony Brook (and later of Poetry for the People in Berkeley) didn't focus solely on African American poetics and poets, June did run her reading series on this premise: what do you get if the only standard is the excellence of the telling? Suddenly, reports were coming in from different generations, different schools, different classes, sexes, and neighborhoods, on how wide and beautiful and varied and complicated the definitions of *America* and *American* happen to be. It was a subtle and subversive idea at a time when the majority of the big reading series held a very narrow definition of what constitutes "good" American poetry.

Both these places turned out to be havens for me, *haven* being defined in this case as a place where you are *seen, understood, challenged*, and *encouraged* at what you are doing as a poet.

These are only two places that come to mind without thinking hard. How many others before us practiced the very old and venerable African American tradition of "making do"? How many unsung church basements, living rooms, community centers, branch libraries, coffee shops, and black-owned bookstores gathered us up, kept (and keep) us going?

I think if you asked a Cave Canem fellow for a definition of the workshop, you would hear some variation of the word *home* sooner or later. This might be a bit misleading, since in fact it's less a house than a tent we've been raising and tearing down every summer for the last ten years. No two summers have ever felt or run the same, and each summer has had its share of joys, angers, and sorrows.

But it's a good idea that Toi had, so clear, simple, and powerful that it spoke to the bruised part of me that had groused to Charles Rowell five years earlier but still didn't fully know what it was looking for that afternoon we all were on vacation in Italy. The same way it spoke to the first twenty-four poets who answered the flyers and ads we posted in the spring of 1996, not knowing the door we all were about to open. By the second evening of that first week, that first summer, everyone knew that this space was special and needed to be preserved. I feel this is the great irony of Cave Canem: the idea was that the space was to protect the poets, when in fact it's the poets who protect the space.

This anthology is a small sample of what has come out of the space we have all had a hand in making. Though it can't give you the sense of celebration, revelation, and healing that comes when all these folks get together in a room and start to blaze away, it might give an idea of what all the fuss has been about: the spoken-word poet tries on the skin of the MFA poet; the MFA poet buffs stanzas with a little street noise; a silence is broken; a hurt or dream or dread is aired; chances are taken; traditions are borrowed, broken, claimed, and reworked. May this surprise and amaze you the way it does us each summer.

I will now break a confidence and tell you that for the last ten years there has always been a moment, usually around the third evening in, after everyone has pretty much gotten travel and the shock of shifting gears out of their systems, when I simply walk around the joint and listen. There's this buzz: someone will be trying to make some deep point about something; somebody else will be agreeing or trying to get a word in; folks will be in the halls or gathered where they've decided the cool spot to hang will be for the year; laughter and music will be spilling from various locations. Books change hands, and drafts are passed around. They're making do.

Toi Derricotte

If I think backward about the success of Cave Canem, for certainly I had no idea that anything like what has happened would happen that first year, I would have to give credit mostly to forces operating of which none of us were aware.

I could tell you I had thought about a writers' retreat for years, had tried to get funding for one and failed in the early nineties; I could tell you about how I met Sarah Micklem and Cornelius Eady at a writers' retreat and loved them instantly for their companionability and honesty—I desperately needed someone to talk with about my experiences as a black poet in academia. Cornelius and I talked for days, knowing from others we were not alone, knowing we needed something better. I could tell you about our vacation two years later, about sitting with them on the veranda in Capri one afternoon surrounded by bougainvillea, a limestone mountain on one side, a city of bells and the green Mediterranean beneath us, and feeling ripe enough to burst open my idea and ask them to share it. I could tell you about how excited they were, how they said yes, and how where I voiced fear—"but we can't get funding!"—Sarah made a bridge—"we can do it out of our own pockets." I could tell you how the next morning, in the burned, buried, and recovered city of Pompeii, in the House of the Tragic Poet, we saw the first "Beware the dog" sign, on a tile in the foyer, a black dog with the words "Cave Canem," and agreed to use this (Sarah's graphic design broke that dog's chain!). That very day we called my friend Father Francis Gargani in New York, and he agreed to let us use Mount Saint Alphonsus monastery the next summer, each fellow with a room overlooking the Hudson. I could talk about everyone's efforts, about good fortune, about Carolyn Micklem, who it seems spent her whole life in the hard work of social justice to gain the spiritual strength and political savvy to direct Cave Canem. I could tell you all this, but I can never show you the most important thing: how, sitting around in a circle on that first night of the first workshop/retreat, almost every one of the twenty-four fellows broke down in tears to the question, "Why are you here?" We poured forth a lifetime of loneliness, hope, and gratitude that we had found each other; we had been given a place that we had longed for, a place of acceptance and encouragement, a circle, a house where our treasures were to be protected and honored. Cornelius and I walked around with our mouths open for days in a profound sense of shock and joy. "Who's in charge here?" we asked each other, smiling dumbly.

I had been writing since I was ten. In all my years of study—from grade school through graduate school—I had never read a black poet. I had never been taught by a black teacher. I was skeptical when I was presented with poems by Langston Hughes when I was sixteen, when I heard the "angry" poems of Haki Madhubuti and Amiri Baraka. There was a suspicion that black people weren't really good enough to be published, to be poets.

My journey as a poet has been to face the locked places in myself that have blocked expression—shame, self-loathing, doubt—finding, inside me, that dead eye that is able to discern its way down deeper than what is stopping it. I felt that among black people, because of some love I saw present in my childhood, even with the torture we did to each other, there was a knowledge of reasons, a whole-making vision. I hoped for a place beyond the graduate rooms where I was afraid to write about race, and a place beyond the communities of black poets where I was afraid to write about anything else. As I taught in programs where I was the only black, that place became more necessary, clearer.

Looking back, I don't think I had the will to do it alone, to push through adversity; I needed the support and validation of a community of like-minded people, which I found in Cornelius and Sarah. Cave Canem is a partnership. It would have been a different place if it had been started by one person. The hardest work for me perhaps happened before I said anything; this was the underground work, the willingness to want this space enough to trust. If Cave Canem is a safe space, it was first of all a safe space for us—not that we always agreed or didn't argue, but we were and are bound by a desire. There's an unsteady steadiness in the number three that made things move and kept them stable at the same time. It bespoke the respect we had for each other, which was a hallmark of the safe space we wanted to encourage. I think the first participants felt this. Maybe part of the success came from our love and trust of each other.

Cave Canem is a community of people who share their most intimate desires during a week-long workshop/retreat; it is also about e-mails year-round among two hundred people, about poetry and day-to-day life, about aesthetics, about everything. One year a fellow had to leave on the first night because her grandmother had died; that same year, the first Cave Canem baby, the first baby from among our fellows, was born.

Cave Canem is a hard place. Safe space is paradoxical. It doesn't mean freedom to write anything without critique. Cave Canem is a place where you are free to risk. This means that you will be critiqued, truthfully, but that you are in a place where you know your critics are on your side, where what you write is deeply important.

Cave Canem is a kind of heaven, yes. It's not just that we are speaking to each other there as black people; it's that we've lived the lives of black poets. We've faced the fears, the hurts, and we're still poets. To undertake and stay with this task, usually so unrewarded, creates a kind of strength and compassion that is enormous.

Ten years. I was completely amazed when a fellow last year said she hoped that Cave Canem would be around when her new baby was grown. It's hard to imagine that this thing that began as a tenuous reaching has gone on to become an established organization with staff and an office in New York, made possible by a Ford Foundation grant. And that this "dream" could go on much further into the future. Toni Morrison says that all writers eventually realize that all their writing is about longing for the ancestors. Cave Canem has helped me to understand my usefulness, between those who came before and those who will come after.

Elizabeth Alexander

What has always been vital to me about the space that Cave Canem makes is that I believe we have truly made room for widely divergent spokes of black aesthetics, poetics, and identity. We live, as Lucille Clifton has said, not in "either/or" but in "and/but." You can see that in the poems collected for this anthology. I always say—occasionally with astonishment—that the Cave Canem community has managed to make a "safe space" for all of us. To invoke Audre Lorde's theories (and imagine

Audre Lorde as a teacher at Cave Canem, as I'm sure she would have been had she lived longer!), the space made for the apparent differences among us makes space for the differences within us, each of us, as we move through the journeys of our lives and our works. That which Cave Canem has affirmed allows this anthology to fairly represent (represent!) all the mighty multivocality of black poetry in the new millennium.

I think of this big book as evidence—no, as manifestation—of this full and glorious moment in African American poetry. This is the state of the art, and it is sound and robust. These poems range so widely in their subject matter and poetic approach that they remind me of what I am proudest of in Cave Canem: that we have managed to encourage and nurture the voice distinct and that the work does not succumb to received or invented doctrine. The faculty poems in this book set us up to understand that we are coming from many different places and that our community has always been multilingual, variously political, multi- and vari- and distinct as we commune under the metaphysical canopy that is blackness.

We have done something important that will last.

Por fin, I repeat the words of Mendi Obadike's poem (which is itself explicitly, stylistically multivocal): "I feel completely drained. The desire to know more." I would add, to describe my own condition: the desire (and yes, it is desire) to feel more and hear more from these poets who together make this a necessary community, not just Cave Canem with a line drawn around it but rather the wild wooly (yes!) universe of contemporary black poetry. This anthology thrills me, makes me say Yes! Teach! Word! Preach! And once again, YES.

Harryette Mullen

I am grateful to be associated with the diversity, innovation, and respect for tradition that Cave Canem allows and encourages. The idea of a designated space to dream, speak, and write poetry is implicit in the organization's name, referring to the ancient ruins of a poet's house that Cave Canem founders Toi Derricotte and Cornelius Eady visited during a tour of Pompeii. As African American poets traveling in Europe, they were aware that what is called "black experience" is only a part of the life that black people actually experience. They knew that pertinent experience of black individuals and communities often goes unrecognized and unrepresented in literature, art, and popular culture. They envisioned a productive space where black poets, individually and collectively, can inspire and be inspired by others, relieved of any obligation to explain or defend their blackness.

Cave Canem refers to a sign at the entrance of the poet's house, "Beware the dog," with a mosaic of an iconic canine protecting the space of inspiration and creation. As their dream became reality, Toi and Cornelius found splendid places to house the poets of Cave Canem, including a monastery on the Hudson River in New York and an art school in Bloomfield Hills, Michigan. The result is not black utopia or a poets' paradise but a plausible and portable literary renaissance that has strengthened connections among black poets while also nurturing an expanding repertoire of black poetry; fostering a broader knowledge of black cultural traditions; and creating valuable institutions such as a public reading series, an annual anthology, a book-publication prize, and an archive of recorded poets' conversations, in addition to the original workshop retreat.

Until my introduction to Cave Canem, I had never entered a room that held as many as sixty black poets. That was inspiration in itself: the sight of all of us together, the range of our voices, the clamor of our work, as we wrote and talked and bopped around the clock. (Afaa Michael Weaver introduced a new poetic form, the bop, at a Cave Canem workshop retreat.) As a faculty poet at Cave Canem, I found many opportunities, as Elizabeth Alexander once said, to move "out of my ruts and predictable selves." I have been as much provoked as affirmed by the energy of our gathering. The Cave Canem poets whose work has been most instructive to me call attention to the myriad ways identity might be constructed. Persistently their poems interrogate the constitutive hybridity of African Americans within the multiplicity of American cultures. As a critical interrogator, the poet stands between opposing definitions of blackness, asking pertinent—and impertinent—questions. I have called it a discourse of "other blackness" as opposed to "black otherness." As Toni Morrison remarked about the various shades and nuances of blackness, it "might as well be a rainbow."

I agree with Elizabeth Alexander that the language and labels we use as readers and critics can obscure significant developments in poetry, as well as interesting turns in the work of individual poets. While the international acclaim accorded to a handful of writers of African descent and the constitution of an African American canon cannot be the end of the story, these developments certainly underscore the truth that the work of black writers has "major" impact and "universal" appeal. To my way of thinking, the existence of such canonized authors allows any one of us more freedom to explore within, around, and beyond the permeable and movable borders of any established tradition.

I would say that African American poets today, as during the 1970s Black Arts Movement, are engaged in spirited, sometimes contentious conversations about aesthetics, identity, culture, politics, and their possible interaction in the lives and works of artists. What seems to characterize the current conversation is a greater tolerance of difference, uncertainty, and even confusion in our lives and in our work as poets. We can exist as black artists without hermetic definitions of art or blackness. I believe this attitude is a valuable legacy of black struggle for self-determination. Our embrace of diversity seems to me a consequence of the Black Arts Movement's bold and explicit declaration of a black aesthetic, positing as its foundation the beauty and integrity of black people and cultures. Rather than suppressing formal innovation, the poets and theorists issuing manifestos of the Black Arts Movement insisted that decisions regarding the artist's use of form, content, convention, and innovation should be motivated by the desire to transform the representation and reality of black humanity.

I also find the spirit of poetic innovation in unexpected places within traditions of black writing. It exists not only in the poetry of such African American antecedents as Langston Hughes, Gwendolyn Brooks, Robert Hayden, Melvin Tolson, Stephen Jonas, Russell Atkins, Bob Kaufman, and Amiri Baraka but also in the fiction of Jean Toomer, Fran Ross, Henry Dumas, William Melvin Kelly, Clarence Major, Ishmael Reed, Toni Cade Bambara, and Toni Morrison. It seems likely that Toomer's mixed-genre novel *Cane* and Hughes's montage poems, along with the prose and documentary poems of Brooks and Hayden, have permitted other African American writers to break through boundaries of genre and to authorize innovative or alternative forms. I am thinking of risk-taking passages in notable works of fiction, such as the haunting poetic monologue of the supernatural voice in Morrison's *Beloved*, as well as such inventive works of quilt-stitched fiction as Alice Walker's *Meridian* and Ntozake Shange's *Sassafrass, Cypress and Indigo*. This innovative impulse also can be found in the theater works of Adrienne Kennedy, Ntozake Shange, and Suzan-Lori Parks and the films of Charles Burnett and Julie Dash.

This publication celebrates the occasion of the tenth anniversary of Cave Canem and displays the dazzling diversity of our black rainbow. CC writers, see what we have done! Every poet associated with Cave Canem was invited to submit poems for consideration. While the constraint of space limits each selected poet to one poem, the advantage is that 124 poems from CC-seasoned poets are collected in this volume, which includes faculty poets, first-book prize recipients, and workshop participants.

The anthology will mean different things to different people. Despite the belief I share with our founders and other Cave Canem poets that this organization is intended to support the creative process of the poet and the poetry community rather than to establish "any received or invented doctrine," some readers might regard this collection as simply another exclusive anthology published by a self-proclaimed aesthetic school or literary faction defined in part by the politics of identity. For others it might offer evidence of accomplishment or a glimpse of the possible. For those of us who have entered the protected space that Cornelius Eady and Toi Derricotte envisioned and created, this publication is a virtual homecoming or reunion, an occasion to acknowledge and appreciate our individual and collective survival as poets. It may become an occasion for actual reunions as the poets published here meet again at public readings of these poems. In the pages of this book, as in the many rooms of the Cave Canem poets' house, I find writers cultivating traditions, committing transgressions, and contemplating just about anything that might be imagined between those divergent positions. This anthology, as selective as it is, offers—yes, as Elizabeth Alexander affirms—a tantalizing sampler of "the mighty multivocality of black poetry."

Gathering Ground

M. Eliza Hamilton Abegunde

For Mairead

(after seeing Gable's End, *1 April 2002, at Ragdale)*

Every part of the world has a door of no return.
Some where once, or even now as you read this,
a mother does not wave good-bye to her child.
She does not want to waste the movement.
Instead, she runs to the child before anyone can stop her,
cries into her mouth and rubs the last tear into her left eye.
As long as this child lives she will see only her mother's grief
and taste its salty bitterness through every passage in her life.

My own mother passed this gift to me: the ability to simultaneously
lose my country, my self, my secure knowledge that I
owned the world. She made me promise not to wave good-bye
to things I could never hope to reclaim, like my name.
Once whispered with pride by priests the day of my birth,
it is lost forever. I spit it into the Atlantic my last crossing, hoping
one day I would find it. But, I have not come that way since
and it has not called me back.

Some where, in Ireland or Senegal, or the United States,
people pass through darkness, every day afraid, hopeless,
naked and shaken by what has been done and what will still
be done in the name of satisfaction. They can no longer prepare
their children for this journey, or teach them about their own.
The children have learned History from books and movies
and know all there is to know.

At this moment, the woman you hear crying is my mother,
or perhaps she is yours. She is probably the mother of every
woman we have ever known. After so many centuries, she is tearless.
She is afraid her grief will be forgotten. She believes we have all
abandoned her, and is praying that one day we will return.
But she is too tired to wait for us to take up her life with our own.
At the top of the stairs, she has left her memories in a drop of blood.

Opal Palmer Adisa

Peeling Off the Skin

i—nat turner as ghost

i would do it again
plot and plan
and kill too
if pushed
would confide
in my betrayer
hoping to win
his heart
to his own
heart beat

> i would do it again
> work my way
> through the hatred
> cover my skin
> with promise's voice
> squeeze through the
> fear until i find
> a breath in which
> to seed one dream

yes
i would do it again
and again
until i see a glint
of a smile snagged
on doubtful lips
and for one black child
to glance unshackled
at the moon

> i would be the ghost
> that prodded their steps
> to head north

i would be the wind
that called them to
my bosom

yes
i would do it again
and i do

ii—nat turner as purse

pressed against
her body
my smooth searing
is the ache
that is her heart
      since she came south
           wife to a man
                who loves breaking things
      she has long been shattered
          shards glued into newness
now he presses
my thighs to her chest
me   a man made fugitive
      we must both endure
          his caresses
      revenge and perversion
          this impotent voyeur
          the husband
who sometimes
      goes to her bed
      lawfully assured
          she will bow down
afraid to run
afraid to be free

but she
lives the underground
railroad
     through   me

i come   between
     them

my skin   the wall
that damns their offspring
through whom
i live on
      and on

iii—nat turner as lamp shade

in destroying
he illuminates
blinded by my blackness

my skin lights
     the freedom
he can never penetrate

           i am the runaway
           god in his parlor

           listening to the talk
my skin stretch taut
enduring the heat
     of the flame
          licking my time

his habits
stored in my hue
next time
i will know
     next time

each night
he sits to read
     his eyes grow dimmer
         by how i shine
           a memory
           that will never fade

Elizabeth Alexander

When

In the early nineteen-eighties, the black men
were divine, spoke French, had read everything,
made filet mignon with green peppercorn sauce,
listened artfully to boyfriend troubles,
operatically declaimed boyfriend troubles,
had been to Bamako and Bahia,
knew how to clear bad humours from a house,
had been to Baldwin's villa in St. Paul,
drank espresso with Soyinka and Senghor,
kissed hello on both cheeks, quoted Baraka's
"Black Art": "Fuck poems / and they are useful,"
tore up the disco dance floor, were gold-lit,
photographed well, did not smoke, said "Ciao,"

then all the men's faces were spotted.

Lauren K. Alleyne

The Taste of Apples

These days there is speculation; they say it was not an apple Eve held to Adam's mouth
and ground against his teeth; it was a fig, they say,

maybe a mango, perhaps a pomegranate, a plum—fruit more exotic and tempting,
more worthy of the Fall. I know apples, polished

skin like blood like wine like war binding tight the white flesh, the black pits
pressed into the narrow center sleeping like sin like sex

like hunger. They say Paradise was tropical, filled with sultry days and balmy nights too unlike
the brisk air, the chill autumn winds needed for apples

to thrive, to come to full fruit. They say it comes down to the geographic impossibility.
I know apples, the way the taste of them knots

the tongue in thick accents, the sandy bite, the sharp sound of separation and the jagged hole
it leaves, the tempered flow of juice of tears of sweetness.

They still say that Eve should have known better, been wiser; should never have strayed,
or disobeyed her creator's command. But I know apples,

the way the first bite sticks in the throat, the dark rush of knowing, the heady flavor, the echo of
the serpent's hiss, saying *taste, taste and see.*

Holly Bass

seven crown man

I am the seventh son of
a seventh son, the last one
a seventh son, the last one
my line comes from bless'd earth
my line comes from bless'd earth
a blueblack star marked my birth
I am the seventh son of

a blueblack star marked my birth
a razor blade cut my course
a razor blade cut my course
no one found the afterbirth
no one found the afterbirth
could be better, could be worse
a blueblack star marked my birth

could be better, could be worse
got what old folks call "the touch"
got what old folks call "the touch"
some men fight against their fate
some men fight against their fate
couldn't tote my blueblack weight
could be better, could be worse

couldn't tote my blueblack weight
or bend the notes so pretty
or bend the notes so pretty
my blues travels heavenbound
my blues travels heavenbound
men cry when they hear its sound
couldn't tote my blueblack weight

men cry when they hear its sound
brine and gin and Georgia clay
brine and gin and Georgia clay
one look makes grown women sin
one look makes grown women sin
my blueblack eyes, coal black skin
men cry when they hear its sound

my blueblack eyes, coal black skin
I pick up where he left off
I pick up where he left off
Night is mister mystery
Night is mister mystery
don't you try to look for me
my blueblack eyes, coal black skin

don't you try to look for me
I'll be gone come daybreak new
I'll be gone come daybreak new
wait and see, these bones fly free
wait and see, these bones fly free
seventh son of mystery
don't you try to look for me

"Seven sevens" is a poetic form created by Cave Canem fellow Kate Rushin consisting of stanzas of seven lines in a repeating pattern, with each line having seven syllables. A poem of seven linked stanzas is called a "seven crown."

Venise N. Battle

Bop Poem

It's said the way to a man's heart is his stomach.
But I been smotherin' chicken and bakin' biscuits
for ten years and my man still use my first name.
Men say they want to feel needed.
Bill collectors stay knocking my door.
I ain't got to whine to let him know his place.

I'd be starving if I ate all the lies they fed.

My preacher says I must submit to my husband,
quit my hardheaded habits, let him lead.
Ain't no man ever led my life. I shovel my own steps.
The man is the priest of his home, he say.
Yes, and I am the abandoned god, blamed but
still providing salvation when he spoons me.
So who supposed to bow to who?
My knees too old to bend.

First in the kitchen   last in the bed
I'd be starving if I ate all the lies they fed.

They say fear is the beginning of all knowledge.
I know better. Compromise ain't an option.
When I launder his clothes, I tuck a pair of
boxers beneath my skirt. I have learned to dress myself.
St. Paul say, "Wives respect your husbands."
I know husbands betta not bedevil they wives.

I'm a woman with the head of a man,
the savior of my own body.
I'd be starving if I ate all the lies they fed.

"I'd be starving if I ate all the lies they fed": From India Aire, "Get It Together,"
on *Voyage to India* (Motown, 2000). "For the husband is the head of the wife as
Christ is the head of the church, his body, of which he is the savior": Ephesians
5:23 (New International Version).

Herman Beavers

LL. Benbow Relates the Circumstances Surrounding Vernell Spraggins's Recent Ejection from Hell

I have to tell you, kinda business I
run bad characters is just a way of life:
murderers, hustlers, English professors,
U.S. senators, ex-presidents right
alongside jackleg preachers, IRS agents,

telemarketers, and talk show hosts.
And believe me, they gets down to the waiting
room, first thing they want to do is talk
their way out, like some kinda mistake
been made. One fella claim only reason he

was here was cause Saint Peter had done misspelled
his name. My custom is to nod my head,
smile, flash my cufflinks, tell them there's nothin
I can do, but of course, end of the month
I'll have the accountants look into things.

Went on like that for eons, didn't have
no problems . . . Then come Vernell Spraggins.

I was runnin one my best hustles,
sellin Cleveland niggas suits out the trunk
of a deuce and a quarter, tellin them
I was havin a party up round Hayden
Avenue way. Now, it's true I tried to

trick the boy out his license, tried to
get him to sign over his life. But that
wasn't no cause for him to do what he
did . . . Looka here, don't be try'na be
no lawyer. If ever a nigga got what

he deserve, it's Vernell Spraggins. No, don't
ask me for no details. Suffice it to
say, I ripped up that fool's contract first chance

I got. I remember like it was last Tuesday:
our mutual parting of the ways come
on account of a can of 10W40

motor oil, a jar of strawberry jam,
two greasy pork chops, Nadinola face
cream, some baby powder, a stick five and
a half foot long, and not a lick of good sense.

Oh, and did I mention my wife?

Michelle Courtney Berry

Miranda Remembers Cuba, 1974

I.

Right before my mother burned the house down,
she tended the roses. Each day that summer, she came wearing the
pale yellow dress, floppy hat, and holding the red toolbox.
If I was in the yard, she'd yell:
Miranda, me voy para la pega, which was a big joke between us,
because she was pretending to leave for an office in Havana.
We were the work—the house, the loud children, the inscrutable father.
The pleasure was in the roses.
In the year Castro said, *After fifteen years of Revolution,*
women's rights are an arena in which we are still behind,
my mother's flowers bloomed.
Everywhere the pink Monticello shrub roses shed their frosty skins.
In the garden, zinc-colored J.F.K. tea roses chortled.
On the patio, geranium-red Floribunda roses spat through cracks.
Running the trellis of the house, the scarlet Altissimo climbed.
In the garden, my mother would push the trowel deep,
deep into the ground around the bushes,
elbow-high gloves gargantuan on the slender arms,
head tilted like a sunflower, legs spread,
and the sharp sucking against the teeth—
the hiss when she forgot the danger of roses.

II.

On the last day of the killings, the fields burned.
All around, the terror of chickens, some headless and running,
others on the metal tables—where the hardest part of all—
much harder than the chopping of heads (which was really quite routine),—
was the pulling of wing feathers and hairs from the anus.
The easiest part?
Chopping the oil gland out, halving the chicken
and clunking the heart and lungs into the silver bowl.

III.

The morning it happened, the day, up on hind legs,
the sun, hot as a whip, clouds rolling in, paella burning the stove.
All the roses were cut down.
Hundreds and still hundreds of flaming heads jutting from the red wheelbarrows
and my mother, standing in front of the house, her hands turning clothespins
over and over, her face blank.
In the punishing heat, the blush-stained blossoms dripped.
The sky pulled back, everything
black.

Tara Betts

For Those Who Need a True Story

The landlord told Raymond's mother that twelve dollars
would be deducted from their rent for every rat killed.
She sends her son to the store for a loaf of Wonder Bread
and five pounds of ground beef. Young Raymond
returns with bread & meat that she tears & mixes inside
a metal bowl. Mama seasons this meatloaf with rat poison
pulled from the cabinet beneath the sink. Well done,
meat sits steaming in the middle of the kitchen floor.
Then the scratching scurries. The squeaking begins
and screeches toward the bowl.

Raymond describes the wave of rats like a tidal crash
covering the bowl, leaping over each other's bodies,
then the dropping, the stutter kicks.

A chorus of rat screams rambles through Raymond's ears.
Keening, furry bodies tense paws against churning guts
as they hit cracked linoleum until an hour passes.
Silence sweeps away the din in death's footsteps.
The mother's voice quivers in her next request.
Raymond, help me count them.

They waded through these small deaths with rubber gloves,
listened to the thump of each dead rat as it rustled against
the slackness of plastic bags.
Raymond wanted to stop counting,
but Mama needed to save a dozen dollars
wherever she could
if they wanted to finally leave the rats behind.
After the last rat was counted, Raymond handed
the bag to the landlord as proof. *Here.*

Enough rats to skip the rent for three months.
Enough rats to avoid the fear of sweet sleeping
breath leading to bitten lips.
Healthy children wrapped in designer dictates
cannot describe Raymond's fear of rabies,
the smell of poison rotting from the inside out,
the scratching inside the walls at night.

Those children
should find soft lives
that drop pendulums in their dreams
and never tell another story
about the ghetto
until they've had to count rats
with their hands.

Angela A. Bickham

Spirit Led

for Levi Pollard

Marse said nobody, but nobody
could eat from his pear tree,
but I did.

At dawn, when the grove was still
brown and dusty from the night,
I ate.

I climbed a tree each morning
so's to find one sweet fruit hidden
behind the inner leaves.

That morning, sitting high in Marse's
forbidden tree, I saw
the spirits move.

Out of the corner of my eye,
past the lobe of my left ear,
the spirits began their trek.

In a drifting smell of swamp,
the orchard leaves began to dance
to low moans syncopating as one.

In the wake of my fifth bite
of pear, two women, a visiting cousin
and Marse's new wife, were killed.

In the wake of my eighth bite
of pear, Marse's house
was set ablaze.

After my tenth and most feeble bite,
those spirits began their movings again
back from whence they came.

I smelled swamp and fruit and smoke.
I smelled hogs and blood and unshucked corn.
I smelled the spirits moving.

The core of my pear dropped
to the ground. I fell
feetfirst from that tree myself

and followed the spirits' trail

disappearing into the morning.

Remica L. Bingham

Marchers Headed for Washington, Baltimore 1963

On Sunday—the amen-scent of fresh meat, apples
bearing nutmeg, collards simmered vinegar-sweet.

For days my father's mother let dawn rub
the back of her neck and shoulders, rising
in time to see the moon.

On Monday—fried chicken battered
with whole flour and double-A eggs,
seasoned with onion salt and lemon pepper.

Hours later, as shards of light brightened
the darkest spot in her kitchen—the deep
closet-like slit that held glass jars full
of last winter's preserves—she'd leave her work
and enter the bedroom her four sons shared.

On Tuesday—fresh Virginia ham, sliced thick,
sweetened with maple sap turned molasses.

Wiping at the sleep lacing their eyes,
one by one her boys marched
to the closet searching for the starched sets
of hand-me-down Sunday best awaiting them.

On Wednesday—pot roast and hotwater cornbread,
the cornmeal sifted as fine as loose road dust
lifting to settle on trousers and lace socks.

If all was right—each bowtie and collar
securely in place—she would line them up
in seats on the porch—even the youngest,
not yet five—then kneel, daily, offering
brief instructions: *Listen, children, and watch*.

On Thursday—smoked turkey, bronzed with heavy
brown sugar, stuffed with new potatoes and corn.

When the morning cooking was done and more lay
waiting in pots atop the steel stove for the afternoon,
she began assembling plates piled so high
they had to be doubled, covered in foil
and set in brown paper bags, strong enough
to endure fifty more stone-ridden miles.

On Friday—fish and loaves, tanned backs of whiting
and yeast rolls passed from hand to hungry hand
until each passerby signaled enough.

When travelers approached, the first son
to spot them would stand and shout, *Here two come,
Mama*—or three or four, even nine came
into view once. Rushing to the door with arms
outstretched, he'd cradle the plates warming
his small hands, then go to the roadside with her message:
*This is for the journey, my mama said,
in hopes that none of you will ever stop.*

Then the next and next until each child
had taken too many plates to count, all
stocked with plastic forks and thick cloth napkins
used to wipe grateful mouths or wet foreheads
and necks weighted down with sweat.

She fed hundreds that way, never seeing
any face close enough to recall it
clearly, her name unknown by those saying grace.
Her marching—from kitchen to porch, then
steadily back and back again—all but in place.

Shane Book

H.N.I.C. (Head Nigger in Charge): B-Side, Club Remix

Bow wow wow yip-pee yo yip-pee yey, where my dogs at, bark wit me now . . .

—*Lil' Bow Wow*

Bow to the one in the white suit, the Stick Up King
of Jersey City—I got lucky—Miss Ella was a little
girl when I was borned and she claimed me. It was
like that and this was like this. It was like wow
to the dark-skinned shortie in the shiny dress,
she got the floss and the flo and the itchy
shimmy. This was not Normandy where there
are many cows. This was where we had prayer
meeting any time, we went to the white folks'
church and there was no whiskey on the place no, no,
honey, no whiskey, and every morning round the way
we'd say Wow to the crushed-can collector,
yeah, that funked-out guy we down with—
he one street off from cool now, but someone say
coming up he'd buck her down on a barrel
and beat the blood out of her—he was this close
to making Bronx Science. They should know.
My owners, my people, my old mistress, wrote me
a letter telling how terrible it was at a dance
one night when a tall, gauchy American mashed
my toe. They say I made a sound that sounded like Yip,
I think his name is P, I think his Q is—who axed
to join the alliance anyway? I mean I never seed
my father in my life but you could always see
the little negro children marching on the levee
on their way to school, blue Appleton Spelling Books
up in front of their faces, chanting: *Both bit the nigger,*
and they was both bad! Much later, they would paint
YO, YOU SMELL LIKE ASS, YO! on the flag
of the High School for the Humanities until one mornin'
the dogs begun to bark, and in minutes the plantation
was covered in Yankees. They were polite, told us:

Non, je n'etais pas jolie. Mais j'avais un teint de roses,
and put food in a trough and even the littlest
gathered round and et. Foremost of these protégés
of Mother was an old mulatto, Célestine. "Yip" was not
her name but she answered to it when we was little G's,
running through the bodega with the buffet that smelled
like piss. Back then my only concern was getting my
leather satchel where I hid Mother's diamonds. That
was what I wanted, that was where I went. *Yey*
was what you wanted, *that* was where you went. You
hit the curtain booth back by the Panama
bananas where the doctors held consultations,
and the suckers for cornrows and manicured
toes hung their shined-out arms, exclaiming,
Oui mon ami, you have made a mistake,
my army don't imitate doorway ass-whuppin
systems! He said she put the money in her pocket.
She said she meant I knows how to raise flax dogs
who wonder where you at, and ladies where you at,
all the ballin-ass niggas in the candy cars,
all the girls in the house that can buy the bar,
lemme hear you say he was on the staff
of *Andrew's American Queen,* a New York
magazine, and he deluged me with poetry, so.
So George, little more than a boy, was allowed
to take charge. He shouted: At some point you gonna see
my slouch as I slow-thug toward you in my crispy
clothes! The family bitterly opposed his going into law,
a southern gentleman had to be a planter
for Virginia was synonymous with dancing
was synonymous with Yes'm, I been here a right smart
while, not: Bark and holla all you want, at some point
I'm gonna fake you to the bridge! I mean at the time dueling
was not very popular. Everyone knew "Wit" wasn't all
it and a bucket of chicken, you had to have game
and a platinum chain to step to this. And besides, at times,
she developed *les boutons* or pimples on her face.
Me, I got my nameplate etched in the corner lecture booth
at Cokie's, the Glock scholars taking constant
dictation. Several claimed their fathers were Sicilians
who came up the river as beggars on pack boats
selling oysters, bananas, apples. They sailed to

Paris for medical treatment. That was where *they* went.
They was a box with eleven hams in that grave.
It didn't bother me, no sir. I been dressed in deep
mourning for over a year. *They* wanted her to be perfect—
for when a sugar planter walked the streets
of New Orleans with his cottonade britches, alpaca coat,
panama hat and gold-headed cane, he was the King of
Creation. To all he would quietly declaim, Now hear this,
it's the mad bling in my pocket, jingling, now hear me
dismiss this classic witness defense quick as a weekend
trip to Vegas, city of red-roofed portopotties, bean-shake
slushies and more ice than you can graft to the fender
of my gold Escalade. But it didn't bother me none, no sir.
Most nights I fell asleep wearing earrings made from old
gutta percha buttons, tiny baskets carved from the shells
of large pecans, I didn't care. Plus, I had to check
on my snakes. The one called slavery lay with his head pointed
south, the one called freedom lay with his head pointed
north. I knows how to grow a snake. You grow it,
it's grown, you pull it clean up out the ground
till it kinda rots. And all night the children's chorus lays
the chorus down: *Both bit the nigger, and they was both bad!*
And in the cobblestone streets some Pimp King
of Something be shoutin', Now hear this, I gotta bounce now,
I gotta ounce now—watch it, this big dog is leashless—

Angela Brooks

Crossing Over

On Saturdays twicedamonth after a breakfast of pancakes and sah-shees we went to visit the sick and shut-in or the well and shut-out (of a right mind). We boarded the city bus toting bags of warm food. Greens usually or straight-out-the-garden peas, a miniature skillet of cornbread, and a tomato. Old rags and bleach to rid a house of the unmistakable stench of sickness and death or from a mind too far gone to detect funk. Grandmama would clean from the front of a house to the back, serve food, pray over and rub down a sick body, or whatever else each case called for. In the beginning I could stomach all except those when death was surely at hand. Along with the family we would circle the bed praying singing and summoning the death angel to come on straightaway and take a suffering soul on to glory and if he was going in the other direction it was pleaded that the Lord hammercy on him. After the first crossover I ax Grand-mama aint she scared of dead people and stuff and she say naw baby and you needn't be afred either. It's the ones left here you better be scared of.

Derrick Weston Brown

Thirty Mile Woman: Sixo's Song
From the Sweet Home Men Series

for Toni Morrison

I ask
the wind for
guidance. In
this place
the trees know me now.
Earth is still earth
and black-eyed Susans
do not differ
so much
from African
violets.
They want me to speak
the tubob talk.
Stop
the dancing,
so I may not
find myself.
When I am lost
you find me.
Gather me
when I am pieces.
Gather me.   Love

the pieces that
I am.
Give me back to me
in all the right
order,
friend of my mind.
I have
asked permission
of all creation
to let us meet.
I would walk
any
length.
Time is your
hard breath
in the field.
I move
when the wind
wills it,
we have tomorrow and today.
Thirty mile woman,
meet me at the crossroads.

Jericho Brown

Detailing the Nape

It's our first summer at Grandmother's and, after our showers, she inspects the dark condition of my sister's neck, declaring it filthy. *You're not cleaning right. We've got to get that dirt off you.*

I peek through a cracked bathroom door as she and my ashamed sister wait over the tub until running water grows hot enough to kill bacteria. My sister kneels under the rush, a sinner prepared for baptism, while Grandmother scrubs as religiously as she scours the toilet each Saturday.

Grandmother breaks to wring and squeeze the purification towel free of water, soap, and a bricklike, muddy dirt. *Child, all that noise ain't necessary. If you could see this nastiness, you'd be thanking me.*

Seeing my sister's distress, I open the door wide. *M'dea', I think that's blood.*

Grandmother quiets and bandages my sister well. *I'm sorry, baby, I didn't know you was that black.*

Toni Brown

Dreadlocks

See
these ropes of hair
This is how
it would have grown
on my head
in the bowels of a ship
long ago

Understand
we dark still living
who crawled or
were dragged
hair matted flat
into this New World
would have been
dreadful

Gloria Burgess

Blessing the Lepers

on the bluffs at Kalaupapa—Molokai, Hawaii

There, tears return, stinging
my cheeks, seep through me
and other presences: rust-red bluffs
that stain a blameless sea and ironwood,
almost impervious, wrested, too,
from its native soil.

Uneasy wind and charred grasses
carry their sighs, the breaths of lepers
brought here in bitter droves against their will.
Hundreds whose sole hope was family
who loved them more than home.

All people want a witness, silent
or loud: this godforsaken colony
beside a mouth of sea, forced settlers,
speaking of themselves to themselves
save for disturbed whispers
and floating cries, worrying the air
from east to west, troubling missionaries,
God, a Father, who bound his future
to this litter of daughters fathers mothers sons.

Some say the air is thinner here,
even when perturbed by thick summer rain.
In angry mists, you see them, round hands
reaching, beckoning their beloveds.

Today, the sun burns through marine-white air;
they are here—behind and before me; they are
everywhere. I'm surrounded by innocents,
snared from tender fields, their open faces
astounded distraught summoning still.

I lower my head in reverence and shame,
kneel on this ridge, feel their pain.
Even so, I hang on the boundary—
vigilant in anguish and unattended grief.

C.M.Burroughs

Coil

She wants just outside
the window, strapped
to branches of Magnolia—
chimes, silver-mapped
chimes. She wants east
winds to clap one chime
into another like strands
of ginger-blonde hair
held pony by elastic rope.
She wants sounds pinioned,
melodic as high-voiced
canaries carousing, half-
singing, half-humming
the exact tune her mother's
mother carried over country
mornings . . . canaries—a cluster
of chimes strapped intimately
to the Magnolia tree. She wants
to palm her ears and hear
nothing, not the brain's blood,
not children ruining the old
street, not dishes cracking in the
dishwater, especially not the sea.
She wants Brasilia between
her big and little toes like
overextended monkey
grass coiling uncut. She
wants a teashop with fifty
lines of wordplay to advertise
the russet-walled, slate-floored,
pneumatic-cushioned room.
She wants the living world to be
gray so that heaven is white
and hell black, so she'll clearly
know where relatives have gone
by the color of smudge on their
noses the mornings after they've

died, and where to meet them
when she has slept too long
to rouse. She wants to walk and
be further along than Eurydice
and without a black smudge
laid on the bridge of her
nose, without a husband
without trust. She wants
to make mustard sandwiches
in the kitchen with her
husband set on a paisley
couch and not disappear
for all his looking back,
and not drown in a sea of
spiced anemone and bread
crusts like waves, and not
hear the sea but chimes knock
silver, one into the other,
strapped touching waxen
leaves of Magnolia, flaxen
as the day is long with its time-
coiled, ginger-blonde locks.

Lucille Clifton

[surely i am able to write poems]

surely i am able to write poems
celebrating grass and how the blue
in the sky can flow green or red
and the waters lean against the
chesapeake shore like a familiar,
poems about nature and landscape
surely   but whenever i begin
"the trees wave their knotted branches
and . . ."   why
is there under that poem always
an other poem?

Taiyon Coleman

Sister

It is three months
before you tell me
that you are pregnant,
and I give you names
of clinics and sterile places
where saving your life
is easy, and people will agree
that it is your choice
to straddle a table
like a cheerleader to split
your thighs wide, so they
will never ache from straightening
your back so that others
won't notice your titties
sagging even with a nursing bra.

You refuse my offer,
and we fight over your
foolishness thinking love
can come in a *redbone*
that carries a college football
all the way from Evanston, Illinois.

It is six months before
we speak again, and your
face is round eating heavy strawberries
draining in kitchen paper towels.
Your pants, unzipped and rolled down,
hug your hips, and we barely
make eye contact. Through peripheral
vision, I watch you carefully bend
your back to safely reach the seat.
You kick off your high-top Filas
worn over like hallway rugs
and out of style because you can't
buy new ones. They are the only
shoes that fit your feet swollen
as holiday walnuts, and I think
to myself that you have never
looked more beautiful.

Lauri Conner

Twelve Year Poem
for Aunt Charlie

I want to make her name a litany Charlie B
a gospel to read but I have never been
one for church so instead I'll tell the story:

her father blue black and neck rope burnt
named his sixth child after himself and in 1926
Mississippi she needed to be as hard and heavy

as her name   as dark as her Choctawed mama
who she would later have to become she would
later be mama to those children   sisters

brothers   one or two years younger in places
where cotton dander and red clay mold you   and she
would dream of escape migrate north like the rest

of the broken   like the rest of the battered and bruised
she would wander to Chicago and smooth sounds
of esquires rotaries she would lindy hop her way

into a marriage that left her marred and barren after
the first child   it's no secret in my family that choice
and consequence weren't always options   and he hit her

the way her father hit her mother   he hit her
on their first night of married life and whispered in her ear
there was a time I was tender remember the fields

as he reaped everything he could from her gentleness
raping her for the second time—the first had been in the rows
of cotton in the midst of her thirteen year bloom—this is

of no importance in light of how small the world really is
and she went to work manufacturing lines of general foods
where she punched time until they forced her to retire

and in giving up work she opened her backyard bar
where they would come for their six pack nights
and they knew if they stumbled down her alley in the middle

of the night her light would be on for them bright
with a hot meal waiting   a pallet on the porch for the drunk
I later found was my great uncle Jimmy   She had become mother

again taking in strays a lover a man married and monogamous
in his lying   and they would mark time by the coming and going
of his body his children   and the things that naturally come

they marked time for twenty-five years and none of us knew he had a wife
until we were old enough to understand that Charlie would never marry
him   and in that he could not leave the woman who did   *my heart*

is broken   he tells my mother over the distance and she
grieving also hears it   *we all wish she was here* she says
and crying for what we had all wished in mourning

when she received the call of his death   a month later
than Charlie B to the date and hour   the heart is fractured
into chambers   and even then   fractured more

Curtis L. Crisler

Robbing hoods

We were hot iron rods in the hot summer with steel thoughts—
girls and boys, mean and looking for means. We gathered brown

paper grocery bags and left Delaney in numbers of twenty or less.
We could make magic in those hot days by being ghetto kids with

a purpose. Our purpose and gonads and stupidity for inspiration
inspired us to win the world before we died. We hit housing

districts with neighborhood watches—those block party houses
that had green green green lawns in the front and back yards

and yellow glow night lamps that automatically turned on at dusk—
dream homes we dreamt to have one day. We were like stairs,

ages four to nineteen—all cohorts in the peasant art of robin hooding

fruit trees and grapevines. Most times little green apples were sour
and fought against a report with our stomachs but we paid no attention

to our parents who said, "They'll give you the shits." We grabbed
the little green apples and the ones with red spots. We had lookouts

in the alleys and the tall kids jumped the fence and the runners ran
with the bags. Peaches were easy. In the graveyard we had no trouble

getting peaches from the dead. We only had the *Green Man* and his
myth spooking the premises in that gray, old toolshed we'd scope out

when jumping the fence, hoping we did not hear the door creak.
We all knew how fertile soil of decomposing bones made peaches

sweeter. Apples were harder to swipe because of guard dogs and brick-

colored security fences. We beat grapes off of vines like Ernest and Julio
and had access to kick ass up the alley like Jessie Owens—even the four-

year-old project kids knew when to run—escape was tattooed in our genes,
man. If "The Man" jammed us in, black kids were streamer blurs

like scattering cockroaches when a light-switch was turned on
and scatter we cockroached. In projects, we returned triumphant,

with brown paper bags full of the fruit. We'd wash off the sour
grapes and the green apples and the hard peaches we had not eaten

on the way back with someone's water hose. We passed out fruit to
the absentee hoods, to our family members, an aunt's current boyfriend,

and saved small stashes for later if the raid was hot and vibrant. Life faded.

TV, toys, and getting caught were small pits. We were passion and guts
and stupid 'cause we were pumped, full force, on that carpe diem thing.

Teri Ellen Cross

Haint

(based on a CNN.com newsbrief)

science tells me
you are still whispering
inside my bones
that years from now
cut me to the marrow
and microscopes will read
the rings of your insistent story
no matter the inconvenient
coupling of timing and desire

no amount of dilation and suction
hemorrhaging and fever
could've erased you nor
the pulp of your carved initials
made with the solid grasp
of a still-forming hand

even now when the bloody show
disappoints our sharpening hunger
do you still cling or are you willing
to let another call my womb
home?

Traci Dant

Standing Ground

My father's land
is gone.
All I have left
are his rods and reels.

On a boat
in quiet water,
I cast
and cast.

My arm, the arm
of all our fishing generations,
who knew land could be sold
from under you.

Our standing ground is here
upon the waters
where no man can move
your feet.

Kyle G. Dargan

Search for Robert Hayden

for Charles Rowell

The garage has not been allowed to breathe
for months now. The smell of moving,
uprooting, cures in the arid Texas heat—
scents that cannot be romanticized, but must be
handled carefully so that no boxes topple.
We are looking for "The Middle Passage,"
first we must clear a walking path.
Books yelp like kennel pups through holes in their crates,
books that are no longer books
but subheadings in chimeras of collected poems.
Next, Copacetic   Victims of the Latest Dance Craze—
all originals baring signatures
like birth certificates. Clifton, no gray.
Komunyakaa, w/beard. Eady,
looking young as the lost member of New Edition.
Most out of print and born before I was pressed
in flesh. The past presented, Hayden is still hiding somewhere.
Putting an ear to the walls doesn't help, this year-old house
barely knows its own nooks and stashes.
Hell, round them all up—in minutes
we'll be standing knee deep in
the unselected poems of black literature.
This is how we will find him:
on our hands and knees
combing over flailed books—seashells
beneath a forgotten tide.
Occasionally we'll wrench something up,
not what we are looking for, and read it anyway.

Hayes Davis

Carapace

I.

The hand on my father's back is curious
even as it tries to comfort. What is the essence
of these bones that feel like rocks under a tent,
shells under a blanket on the beach?
Where will I go with this jagged feeling,
new knowledge of his insides? My mind

will keep these stones. Can I look closely,
notice crag and crevice, or am I able to look
at all; are my eyes too close, the feeling
too new, too sharp? What will the stones
do in my stomach, in my mouth?

What kind of archaeology is this? Island Beach
used to be our comfort; soon he will rest there,
stones to sand, sand to water.

II.

Comfort for now is cool washcloths
on his forehead. It is Jolly Ranchers
after days of Thorazine sleep,
a nurse just a little gentler than the last.
Comfort will be tubes removed, an ambulance
home, dressing in his clothes,
drinking from his own glasses, wearing
his own underwear. His house filled with people,
the quiet when they leave.

III.

Comfort is helping him pee, or lifting him
onto the toilet, waiting, wiping after his bowels
stir reluctantly. Sitting up with him when he
is afraid to sleep, laughing quietly, writing
the obituary, as if listening to old stories—
his body running cross-country, riding a motorcycle—
will smooth stones, slow time.

Atlantic Coasts

These boys could be in Praia,
I think. Dried sea salt coarse
across their shoulders. They dig
their feet into the sand, chase

glimmers of polished glass
and trail tracks along the shore
leaving smudges like their grandfathers
left on Cabo Verde at this age.

Across the ocean and decades
before, two boys called each other
in Crioulo. I picture the brown
mountains watching from behind,

and the sea washing up smooth
rocks and jellyfish for them.
But they're not in Praia, they're here,
we're all here, in New Bedford where

they dig at the beach with sticks
and face the Atlantic from
the other side. "What are you taking
pictures of?" the boys ask me.

"The beach," I say, and they scatter
sand behind them to collect
their stash. "Take a picture of this,"
the younger one suggests, holding

a twisted clump of seaweed
and goo. The older boy is serious.
He carries stones with important
colors for me to photograph.

Our tie to each other
and to the past is the water.
They do not discover
and uncover bits from shore,

their home, to remember lost
family in Cabo Verde. This
is where they are. This is where
we are. "Take a picture of this,"

the younger one offers, grinning
at the snail peering from its shell.

Kwame Dawes

Tall Man Flies

Gangly man, skin like red dirt,
you have let rip,
a streak of living
across these here United States.

Philadelphia, Detroit,
New York, like a curse,
Missouri, Washington.
When they saw you coming,

they cleared the jails.
Traveling man, it took nothing
for you to pick up
and follow the boy King

into batterings by sticks
washings by spit
beds of stone
crying "Freedom! Freedom!"

'Cause this nothing town
called curfew before the sun
was quite tired of it all
and they would lock you up.

Keep moving, nothing would slow
you down until, bone-weary
some flame of Pentecost
caught you and singed what little

hair was left
and gave you a voice
to preach in iambics
like in the old days.

You've got more years to go,
though the way words are found
has clouded some in your head,
the way thoughts make memory.

But all those years of letting rip
gave you psalms of penitence,
each day offered, a sin forgiven
a new song made, eyes clearing.

I can tell you've been talking
to the dead, the way you are startled
to find me before you, the way you expect
me to know the street you live on,

and every dream in your head
that you have not spoken to me,
but have said to those
you talk to at night.

I follow you to the Atlantic's edge,
then I let you go on ahead,
staring at your gangly flight,
old arms pointing homewards.

Jarvis Q. DeBerry

Juke Joint Josephine

She is blacker than a bruised big toenail,
Tough, scaly, defiant as the blues.
A champagne glass on her gold tooth
Matches champagne-colored shoes.

She laughs. Says my boat can't possibly
Be big enough to plow through her wet sea.
I say, "Drowning? Between hips like those?
Don't think you're scaring me."

Says she's seen my kind and knows me well:
Seditty. Too stiff to get down.
Demands to know why I'm here again
On her broke-down side of town.

It's my fascination with full, round breasts
And the women who carry them proud,
Sweet perfume on sweaty necks,
Blue Bland blaring loud.

I'm Mississippi born and bred
With a big-city education,
Know Ovid, Chaucer, Goethe, Keats
Plus some old Greek conjugations.

But I wants a woman who will send me on
Her most intimate feminine errands
And love me till I start to drop
The g's off all my gerunds.

Toi Derricotte

my dad & sardines

my dad's going to give me a self
back.
I've made an altar called
"the altar for healing the father & child,"
& asked him what I could do
for him so he would
do nice for me. he said I should stop
saying bad things about him &, since
I've said just about everything bad
I can think of &, since . . . well,
no, I change my
mind, I can't promise
him that. but even healing is
negotiable, so, if he's in
heaven, or trying
to get in, it wouldn't hurt
to be in touch. the first thing I want is to be able to
enjoy the little things again—for example, to stop peeling
down the list of things I
have to do &
enjoy this poem, enjoy thinking about how, scouring
the cupboards, I found a
can of sardines that
must be five
years old &, since I was home after a long
trip &, since it was 1 A.M. & I hadn't eaten
dinner &, since there was no other
protein in the house, I cranked it open &
remembered that
my dad loved
sardines—right before bed—with
onions & mustard. I can't get into my
dad's old heart, but I remember that look on his
face when he would load mustard on a saltine, lay a little
fish on top, & tip it with a juicy slice
of onion. then he'd look up at me from his soiled
fingers with one eyebrow
raised, a rakish
grin that said—*all
for me!*—as if he was getting away
with murder.

Joel Dias-Porter

A Love Supreme

> *The mystic path is the path of a Love Supreme.*
> —*Kabir*

1. Acknowledgment

In a room dark
as the inside of an egg
John Coltrane awakens,
imagines a shimmering riff
that would fit
(like the name of the Lord)
on the lips of a kneeling child.
He rises, assembles
his tarnished sax.
Once he loved the sharp notes
a needle played in his veins.
Can his smoke-stung lungs
inspire a higher key?

2. Resolution

If he turns his sax upside-down
it curves like a question mark.
What is a true measure of music?
Notes vibrate at various frequencies.
One melody brings back his grandmother
dozing by a fire in her favorite chair.
But, could a sacred chord diminish
a mass of malignant cells,
can a holy trill
fill a beggar's cup with coins,
could a righteous riff
rumble rain from white clouds?
He takes notes
to resolve this progression
of questions.

3. Pursuance

He grips the mouthpiece
between his teeth
closes his eyes
and tongues the reed
his sax refracts sound
collating chords into colors
the first b-flat floats
black as smoke from a locomotive
rides the silver rails of a minor scale
pulling his remaining rainbow
past the signs of time signatures
around the sharp curves
of a treble clef
down through a kale-green valley of verses
over a wooden brown bridge
pursuing a riff soothing
as sunrays on his naked back.

4. Psalm

Dawn's yellow fingers
crack the black shell of sky,
Trane's fingertips trek
across the brass tracks
of his tenor sax.
He turns
towards the sun
blowing three notes
as one
note of sweat
dots the thick cords
of his neck.
As the sun ascends
its yolk
spills across the horizon,
drenching him
in a bright robe of light.
His head bopping
in a rhythm of revelation,
he hits a riff
that rises into the still morning air
radiant as a prayer.

mug shot pedigree

tall	brown	mid-frame	bald
tree	bag	average	clean shaven
high tower	wood	proportionate	groomed
long		tight	buzzed
elegant	dark brindle	loose temperament	scalped

6'2"

Philipe Roberts, A661126, Black Male
Whelped: 05-07-85, Stud Book: 12-87; Call Name: Phieggy Boo
Tests: [OFA Good 03-17-87, SLT/PRA[1] 05-87, Clear, CS 2644G33F]
[SIRE: Pierre Roberts]
[DAM: Juanita Mackie Roberts]

1 liter	white oak		built	waves
thirst quencher	black strap	thick	boy	
40 ounce	creamy muthafucka		kunta kente	runt of litter
sip of——	jet		mighty joe young	overgrown

deep plum	baby daddy	DMX	
waxed	certified		stud
broad		champion	doo rag

smooth   laid back   shoulder
front   & rear   strong & balanced

Breeder(s): unknown at this moment

---

1. OFA (Orthopedic Foundation for Animals). When a dog is registered with The American Kennel Club, for example, the dog will be given a grade regarding the orthopedic health of its hips and elbows. This is done in hopes of reducing the incidence of canine hip dysplasia in future offspring.

  PRA (Progressive Retinal Atrophy). A disease of the retina and hereditary disorder found in most purebred adult dogs. Diagnosis of the disease is usually made by an ophthalmoscopic examination.

R. Erica Doyle

The Street of Look Behind

I have forgotten your address.
The blue house floats
on an imaginary street.

I make you invisible
to my last mind.

I do not find joy
in your name.

I erase your voice
from my ear's nostalgia.

This makes me
happy
in a way
that is a lie.

I remember some things:

crawling back to you naked over porcupines
selling my qualms and other precious possessions
giving you all the proceeds
ending up broke and unemployed
for a dream
written in maggots.

I paraded in red.
You wore black and laughed
at my lack of style.
I paraded in black.
You tore my garments.

Your skeletal friends
shook their wrist bones
in my face and you agreed.

I could never feed your ghosts
enough blood.

I hid blue in a corner
you opened the box
and threw it at my throat.

Today I don't care
who is to blame.
I can't remember
your address.

In the street
of look behind
the horizon
waning.

Camille T. Dungy

Code

Miss Amy wants me down to the market and see if I can't find fish   *for sale. Two*
bushels to be delivered, but the driver's sick today. Miss hates to waste   *house servants*
on errands, but we'll need the fish come dinner. Mostly scrod and she-crab(*the female*
be the best for my stew) is what I'm hunting for. Folks say I'm   *not to be surpassed as a cook,*
the best girl 'round this place. Miss Amy claims she can't be bothered with another   *washer,*
so today I'll see to errands, scrub clothes, and stew fish, and tomorrow I'll be cook   *and ironer too.*

Can't say as I blame Miss Amy her grip on the house. Heaven knows,   *her husband's a first-rate*
scoundrel, and a groggy fool to boot, Master Jackson was in amongst the 'taters with that   *servant*
girl name of Lena. Promised a kiss and a gold piece for some trick of the leg he saw   *in a tavern*
in his bachelor days. Lena's worked eight years in this house. She ain't seen   *and experienced*
enough to know to keep out of the cellar when the man's breath smells worse than   *ostler's*
britches? Miss caught Lena's left arm, burned the thief's T in the thumb of her right   *hand.*

Cornelius Eady

I'm a Fool to Love You

Some folks will tell you the blues is a woman,
Some type of supernatural creature.
My mother would tell you, if she could,
About her life with my father,
A strange and sometimes cruel gentleman.
She would tell you about the choices
A young black woman faces.
Is falling in with some man
A deal with the devil
In blues terms, the tongue we use
When we don't want nuance
To get in the way,
When we need to talk straight.
My mother chooses my father
After choosing a man
Who was, as we sing it,
Of no account.
This man made my father look good,
That's how bad it was.
He made my father seem like an island
In the middle of a stormy sea,
He made my father look like a rock.
And is the blues the moment you realize
You exist in a stacked deck,
You look in a mirror at your young face,
The face my sister carries,
And you know it's the only leverage
You've got.
Does this create a hurt that whispers
How you going to do?
Is the blues the moment
You shrug your shoulders
And agree, a girl without money
Is nothing, dust
To be pushed around by any old breeze.
Compared to this,
My father seems, briefly,

To be a fire escape.
This is the way the blues works
Its sorry wonders,
Makes trouble look like
A feather bed,
Makes the wrong man's kisses
A healing.

Michele Elliott

Uncollected Ghazal

I used to collect people but now I collect things.
People became unmanageable, so now I collect things.

The easy way out is, I am nothing.
I have nothing, so I collect things.

Like sounds and words and laughter—
The uncollected, I collect these things.

I collect vision and dancing—lines blurring, beautiful.
I have nothing to hold this in, but still, I collect things.

Like rainstorms and broken dreams,
Whispers and eyewinks—these precious things.

I am no one and nothing.
I am everything and urgent. I collect things.

Like silence and tears,
And loss. Oh, these precious things.

I used to collect people but now I collect things.
I have nothing to hold you in so now I collect things.

Phebus Etienne

Music Lesson

for Jehan

Tumbling back to previous summer dusk,
I capture the boy spliced into a writers' retreat.
His father critiqued manuscripts and gave him
jazz lullabies. Raw with joy, the son
improvised a suite and scattered melody
on idle piano as poet read solemn stanzas.
Player startled reader to silence
and his mother rushed to collect him
amid irrepressible giggles of the audience.

Cicadas teased the humid night as I looked for lyrics
to paint his discovery of kiwi,
to utter what a childless poet understood
as she cleaned chocolate from his lips,
to honor desire of a father-to-be who entertained
with chiming keys and talking gadgets.

My lines were earnest melodrama as dawn's
pastel-tinted wings glided into view.
I paced from ginkgoes to firs, circled a pond thick with algae.
Mosquitoes dived to sample flesh, but I didn't
rush from the bites reddening fingers and knees.
Blue jays caucused in leaves, vowing to conquer
berry fields as water rehearsed its verses.
Inebriated in sound, I was relearning wonderment.

Dwarfed by redwoods reaching for morning mist and sun,
I read a mosaic rife with pairs of severed veins.
A doe lies quiet in her thicket bed as a
banana slug inches up a hill damp with dew.
Behind my lids, Jehan is smiling as I replay the baritone
of bullfrogs composing nocturnes among water lilies.

Chanda Feldman

True Autumn

I return to the dead-end
street where I grew up, at the edge of
the county, at the foot of lavish
green hills, with dogwood- and magnolia-
plotted medians, where once a year,
my mother places a five-gallon bucket
of chitlins straight from the deepfreeze
next to the stove's warmth to thaw.
The long chain, slime-gray,
lovingly scrubbed clean of grit.
My mother says it's not true autumn
without eating them, as vital as blood-
rich colored oak leaves. As a kid
I loved the slurp of entrails
slicking my throat, but I never forgot
my white neighborhood friends' tables
set with bowls of lobster bisque
and baguette slices. Contained. Not all
food-juice mixing on the plate.
Over dinner my mother talked stories
of her father stringing hogs
for November slaughter as segue
to discussing black family mobility,
and my father drew imaginary lines
from stomach to mouth, a knife gutting
the hog body. How quickly matter
comes apart, as with words,
how to convey suburban two-acre lot,
where my family feasts on saucy delicacies
while trading superstitions about haints
and spirits and, in the next breath,
discussing protons penetrating solids.
How I used to crave no barrier
between me and other families. I'd pass
through brick and into beige safety—
no jellied pig's feet, no hot combs
smarting the ear, no smell

of oozing chitlins when it's near winter
and too cold to throw open windows
as we did. Each time the house filled
with their sweet stench, I'd cover my nose,
my mother always scolding,
"Some people never eat like this."

Nikky Finney

Stewards

for Cave Canem

The only ones
who still stand before they speak
who memorize their lines by heart
who forewarn
are flight attendants
and poets.

One is tragic
always pointing to where
the oxygen mask will fall.
The other takes her cabin-pressured seat
strapped to understanding:
The idolized air
once loosed
is never free.

Reginald L. Flood

Worship

for Mab Segrest

> *The image I got in my head that day was the image of her face lying in the water, very smooth, with the eyes closed, under the dark greenish-purple sky, with the white gull passing over.*
> —*Robert Penn Warren,* All the King's Men

Miles from this bus bench twisted up from concrete
are live oaks and a rock-filled creek gurgling quiet as church
on Monday afternoon—when the clink, clink, clink of money
from the deacons counting yesterday's protection
for paradise is the final hymn echoing on this street,
far from those boulders and clear water under a simple sky.

The poet gave us this—one white gull against the purple-green sky
reaching across war, empty pages to make loss concrete,
so the distance between body and blood makes sense on the street
even when you can't worship at the altar—because real church
never been easy—that's why this valley offers the sweetest protection
in sycamore silence—far from hallelujahs for heavenly money.

Because the City is there—always there—"Bro where's the money?"
"Cash—some of that energy—don't you want to be sky
bound in jus a sec—then stroll to her—nah, nah baby, no protection.
I like it raw, and your butt sounds damn good slapping concrete.
Three bills to me. Two to her, and my brother it's church
church"—because nothing, nothing needs to be real on this street.

Before asphalt and sidewalks everything was real on this street
adobe dust connected that City and creek without resort money—
just one-day's walk and this sumac and sagebrush church
could be worshipped hard in Latin under the most wild sky.
Those parishioners understood these stars but not concrete
or new shivers between chants about their souls needing protection.

The chalice following the wafer reflects what you need protection
from—that face bouncing off silver that colors this whole street—
twenty, thirty pieces—don't matter—it all ends up answering to concrete

because this City leeches legal tender & money, money, money
chisels away flesh chunk by chunk even under that incredible sky
making all parables in middle age suspect—especially in church

because real revelation always ruptures—making those church
songs echo into gospel over acres of cane without protection
from what you will never understand—the blue of a blank sky
against a looped rope that still dangles over this street
each corpse surrounded by smiling faces holding drinks & money
for a photo that fades into sepia like blood stains on concrete.

Nothing's more concrete than the steeple on top that church
pointing not at folding money or soapbox rapture for protection—
but vision from this street—one white gull scarring the sky.

Cherryl Floyd-Miller

is

1.

in *glyph*, the mind of percival everett's baby ralph asks, "is a photograph always present tense?" as in here I *am*! there you *are*! this *is* us as we are about to . . . as if it hasn't happened. as if we don't know our lives before and after the *is*.

2.

be: show: occupy space: go or come: equal in identity:
signify: belong: exist: remain undisturbed or untouched.

in a flash it all *is*. we are all *is*.

3.

g.e.p. & gio (separate is's) won't
permit picture takers to take them.
steals part of the soul, they say.
but I am sneaky, eye them anyway,
eye their i's for soul, take away
their heats, preserve them in retina,
slip them onto films of *was* until i speak
them again. now, here i am bringing them
into speech about not taking (giving)
pictures. i say, *g.e.p. is: gio is.*
and they are present.

4.

in this picture, i am a bride. i am also a daughter, sister, cousin, in-law, niece, grand child. a four-month fetus *is* inside of me (but you only know because I am telling). i am dancing my first steps as a wife. a skinny man wearing a dufi and sprawling lips is holding me. he is in my eyes. taking me.

i burn this picture. set afire its membranes and shadows. it *is* no more: it *was:* we *were*.

5.

here i speak of it,
signif it for you. disturb,
touch it, retrace its haunt.

it is a picture again. it is.

Krista Franklin

Saturday Nights at the Bug Inn, 1986

Plastic cups watch from divide between
pool room and dance floor. Their golden insides
pulling stingy light down from the ceiling.

Drunk men, eyes hard as wood floors, watch.
Some lean their bodies across pool tables,
one pale arm stretches down the length of stick.

There is no space on the small dance floor.
The smattering of brown bodies here squeezes
into any open space they will.
The bar air swells with sweat and sound,
my mouth fills with my phone number.

The deejay spins almost every word we know:
Ratt, AC/DC, Def Leppard.
Electric guitars climb out of speakers,
and slither into our hips. We are four black virgins
perspiring in the heat of roadhouse.

My voice is caught in the grooves of night.

Like big cats in a forest of antelope,
the few black boys here circle white girls
who sprout from these backroads, smell
of hairspray and floral alcohol of drugstore perfume.

I am here for anyone and no one;
sit in dark corner with my legs stretched on another,
drink water and watch the ritual of torsos
pressing against one another, the mysterious
conversations falling into caverns of ears.
Here, I perfect my *I-couldn't-give-a-fuck-less* face.
Glare at the ones who stare too long.

Inside, I am howling wolf.

John Frazier

A Human Landscape: On Coyotes

It is more difficult than imagined
to trap the sly creatures and believe them

at once to be sly and unsly, not so
unlike those terrible dancehall bodies

which are, after all, only belonging
to other men. Coyotes won't come

in their usual forms of trickery
in torsos where ribs show

and press against skin and fur that displace
with touch. Bodies have a way

of doing this—shifting. And they always
seem, don't they, hurt thing, more and less

dangerous than your own? There will be an impulse
to stop, to begin: *I know how to suffer.*

Deidre R. Gantt

Corner Yard

The Cool Freeze truck once drew the neighborhood
like crack fiends to our honeysuckled fence.
The grown-ups bought banana boats and left

their kids inside our ghetto Disneyland.
This was 1986. My cousins
in Virginia Beach had cable, Pac-Man,

pink lace bedspreads and real mattresses—we
had all outdoors. Soft and yielding blankets grassed
our kingdom, fruit trees like billboards, tempting

us to taste the cherry. I hurled spirals
at the sun that summer, and discovered
spaces blind to mothers' eyes and windows.

I know the scratch of bark between my legs,
the dogwood's smooth deception. Their guilt-stained
flowers ushered winter, the smell of death

in my grandfather's breath and Nintendo.
Next spring, the Cool Freeze truck returned to coax
controllers from our grasp, two by two, then

back to Tecmo Bowl and Judy Blume
and cueing *Inside Seka* to the scene
my mother started watching recently.

Back to my abyss of nappy hair
and peach-pit breasts and blood and boys who laugh
at my chubby, awkward admiration.

Ross Gay

Unclean. Make me.

When the body blooms, you must
put your face to it. Lay tongue
to the lathe, the blessed
lather. Song like marble spun
into silk. The human
loom. The thread limning your lips. Breathe
there. Fill your lungs
with birth's florid shadow. This is the common dream of the living
and dead: not only to meet
the maker, but to taste its sweet. Even God
should know this.

Regie O'Hare Gibson

Zeitgeist 0

When the voice began

Singing was when the fist opened was when
Space failed between hammer and anvil was
When something lifted our hands to our faces
Was when scales fell and we

Named them . . .

Was a querulous light then aching our eyes was
Verb exacting the length of our ears was feet
Religioning their way through intestine toward
some fearful

Damascus . . .

Where messiahs were dancing on smoldering
Textbooks where oracles spoke of the fire to
Come like an embryo prophesy nascent and
Lumbering its way toward

Insurrection . . .

But there was no word yet for insurrection no
Word for a breathless at last no word which
Incanted: let killers be fearful as faith in a church
Built by slave-owning men our books wouldn't
Translate

A barren constitution . . .

Or teach us the phonics of bulleted speech no
Blueprint would show how to build a new brick
To stitch a new tower from us to the voice all
we knew was we needed a tower   a stitching of
Brick back

Into the voice . . .

Zeitgeist 63–69

. . . It was the hour of teargas and napalm—
of monks immolating like huts of saffron
straw—of red fear quaking the grassy knoll—
the bullet the balcony—Audubon and
Allah—It was our cities become crucibles
of ash—and hurricanes of cock ripping rice
women open—It was the hour of knife and
womb razor—The hour of hope impaled
through the rib—

How did we come to this high place of lonely—
What solitary road did we travel to this stone—
What are the names of these scars of our anger—
What do you call this ineffable moan—

We were the great comet come to extinct all
dinosaur watch them fossilize in the after
of our impact and all escaping our fire
would be captured stuffed displayed in
museums so posterity could see what once
ruled but the doubt found us again kept
finding us no matter how our tribe urged
onward it hunted us like a madness slow
and hereditary a deliberate and bitter
alchemy speaking the monsters back into
our knowing

What is the poem of a splintering anything—
What is the prose of a backward tear—
Is there a color for a hi-jacked alphabet—
Why does hope name her immigrants blue—
Where is the scale telling what blood weighs—
What are the increments of non-ness—
Is there a flower named future forgive us—
What is the smell of a doubting hand—
How do you say thirty pieces of silver—
How do you say my country is torn—
How do you say my eyeballs keep melting—
How do you say 13,000 miles from home—
How do you say the nightsticks keep bleeding—
How do you say there's a gun in my god—

Ours was wailing and gnashing of teeth—
ours was escape to a narcotic haze—the
time of fist and faith in the gun in the mouth—
and of tanks rolling into our learning—
it was the hour of the crossroads—when
pacifist and fascist shared the hour of the
tolling bell—of soldiers returning with
faces made zero while banners burned a
ghost of mangled stars into our hands

There is the child who burns like a flag—
Here is the flag that sleeps like the law—
There is the law which laughs like a racist—
Here is the racist living like a martyr—
There is the martyr dying like a president—
Here is a president falling like shrapnel—
There is the shrapnel singing like a woman—
Here is the woman weeping for her child . . .

Carmen R. Gillespie

Talkin' Back to Mama

Broom in hand, she screamed:
"Gal I'll knock your head off
And roll it out the back door."

Hand on hip, I stood defiant.
How far could a broomswept
head go anyway?

Past her greens and cabbages,
through the alley and Daddy's car,
down High Street, over the bridge,

to Norway and my friends,
Snip, Snap, and Snurr.
(We met in Lane Library.)

I could always come back for my body later,
and I wouldn't be like the Easter chickens running
headless 'round the yard after her bloody twistings.

I'd walk out the front door
and show the neighbors
what she did. Keep walking,

hand on hip, to someplace new.
To the fjords, to my friends,
(and my head) in Norway.

Aracelis Girmay

Palimpsest

What is it called,
the word most sadness,
stretched long as trains,
rain on clotheslines,
sheets on clotheslines,
to undo the sun, in a back room,
or under a tree, a tamarind tree,
isn't there a word
for yellow-husk morning
of coke-eyed soldiers
putting gun to daughter's head
and enjoying, serpentine,
the Fuck this child or we will
kill her, and fuck even
your babies and your boys
with our own 5 dicks.

And the father,
letting down his pants,
his hands like rain,
down to his ankles,
his long thighbone,
there is a scar,
it runs so long,
down to his shin,
he, sobbing, naked,
up to the sky,
into her chamber
smell of sweat,
he cannot stone,
no thing will gallop,
it is so quiet
inside his ear
the way she cries
his name

of

prep. **1**. origin or cause: Aaron begets Helen, Laura, Ermine, Christine, Inez, Beulah, and Sonny. Sonny, he died *of* female complications. **2**. material or substance: the house was built *of* bricks and still stands despite neglect. The spit between them was built *of* whipping sticks and switches, tethered straps and 100-proof whiskey. **3**. belonging or connection: my mother gave me the gelatin prints *of* her growth. **4**. identity or close relation: my daughter says she wants nothing *of* me. **5**. removal or separation: what happens to daughters cut out *of* mother's milk? **6**. reference or direction: because *of* this. **7**. partition, classification, or inclusion: my mother's walls are full *of* salt and pepper shakers. I collect this sort *of* story. **8**. description, quality, or condition: girls *of* ten remember things. **9**. time in relation to the following hour: it was a quarter *of* and half past.

Michael S. Harper

Goodbye Porkpie Hat

> Pres's signature   his moniker   the many mf's
> he could verify   your poetic character   one trait
>
> you brought with you into the world
> (this wasn't caught on film   though Dexter
>
> had that great laugh   composite characters
> is what white filmmakers see blacks   is)
>
> yet Mingus caught Pres's stride in ballads
> easing of the glottals   his very song   eclipsed
>
> in the high registers   down low in Kansas City
> airchecks were breathy   loved the dancers   Savoy
>
> kept us out of there except on kitchen mechanic
> "low wage" days   fraternizing was bad for blood
>
> Pres's eyebrows had this expression when Lady sang
> (they didn't talk for years   then one night
>
> like old times   he slipped her sultry embrace
> carried her along   whatever broke them up
>
> as pals   was the best dish in Minton's pantry
> both from musical families   the old man strict)
>
> how do you get people to pay attention   blues
> can't be captured on film   on hotel walls   takeout
>
> it's attitude   Mingus caught that poetry only
> discernible in quality   once in a lifetime   pres

Duriel E. Harris

Phɵu

I will answer you, and will tell you great and hidden things that you have not known

—*Jeremiah*

i.
I want to blow my brains out. How many times have I said this:
Out, taut smog. Out, shadow. Coarse white cloth, billowing.

phɵu, the pilot breathes in sleep.

clean.

what is real is my capacity to damage and to heal.
what is real is my choice between two
and the way I oscillate, measuring.

ii.
once I sent a woman into the street to wait.

4 A.M. Brooklyn heat. She called the cab and went down; I canceled it. From the window, I watched her waiting and pacing, smoking a cigarette nervously, then another. Brooklyn trees are known to block streetlamps and passageways. Outside you could not see what moved until it was upon you.

Now and again a hoopty livery cab would chuckle along, rolling its heavy engine: *Goodie-bye*, it would say like mythical Ibo flying away, leaving her put cause she didn't have no wings, just feet, and they were swollen from salt and cracked and pudgy the way feet can be like sausage, the ends of things stuffed into skin. I watched her from upstairs and went down, kindly asked if she'd like me to call again because I would, because even though I was sending her away something in me wished to be kind. Still she waited, out in the street flicking a cigarette staring into the maw of Murder Ave. She dug around the tree bricks with her piggish feet, clawing at shit. For how many minutes can a woman wait for a cab in the 4am dark away from the city's yellow zooming? *Phɵu.* She walked to the corner and on. I

didn't feel bad. We both knew she was stupid to hoof it toward
Fulton Street that late: anyone could snatch her out of the air and
bludgeon her head into suffocation, balled point, stain. Did I sus-
pect she would hail a drunken cabby and ride hellbound home?
Did I care? She deserved. She had earned it and the world could
give it to her. Yes, we could give it to her.

iii.

> *Satisfaction is being where you belong, just warm enough,*
> *just full enough to forget where your skin ends and the world begins.*

iv.
On the screen, the 4-year-old boy squirms
beneath the man. His red cap, his bicycle:
caught. Little red riding hood: the man
opens his fly just enough to get it out,
get it in.

> *O veil of the sanctuary.*

The man's ecstatic peeling rips, from rafter to board.
This time, red is eaten by the woodsman. There is no wolf, just me.

pheu.

francine j. harris

Coward

(denotation)

I'm telling you it's not like you disappeared, that's not the point.
The point is you didn't vanish, or trail off or come all out in your hazen gown.
The point is you brought it on. fifteen boy, with your dropping stone,
the pull your own, the i-skip-railroad-tracks
and moon ties over the city. the point is you could have, Sully-eyed.
You could have rinsed with water or staved it off, instead
you left the bowl alone, heeded the time's roadside signs.
The point is you took it upon your self to bring that out and leave it out to dry.

They say . . . well, they say nothing about you, Mr. DogEared,
because you disappeared. Side rocking and silly toed,
Vanish man across the sideways bricks of buildings, hesitant.
They say—they say nothing because when they remember your name,
it's some other man they remember, not some other man, but some other man.
So it isn't how you came or jumped on what bus, long ride trainside
to find other vacant buildings to house up and nod over,
it's that there in your appearance, you always disappear.

If I had to tell you, I'm saying it's the pulley mechanics of dodging,
you soggy tongue. It's just that nice. just that calm
and vapid gunloaded machismo, it's just that watch the window all night until
it disappears off into that phosphorescent fade and slip shod and finish
what you started, Gooseyneck. It's that dream you gobble, Gingerbake man,
broiling off the daily risk of disapproval. You're so safe in delirium,
no one's beefsteak without your street clothes. Doorag Monster, prickly Scarbum.
You're that magic trick who never thinks to cheat. Never has to be around to
believe in anything. oblivious needlework scratching at your neighborhood face.
Sick of you, bloated Proper Speech. They say, they say you're sleeping.
They say leave you alone, you're poor, harmless. harmless. harmless.

Reginald Harris

MT in Solitary

Life is ruled by Spaces,
even I learned that much:
In a square of light 20 feet around they
want an animal. Outside the ropes
battles point to incarceration, a cell, alone,
walked off at 6 by 9.

      It don't
matter. I'm used to
shadowboxing, am the shadow
they all placed bets on,
an iron cup bulging with their fear.

          What choices did I have?
Boxed-in from birth by the Boogie-Down,
"freedom" what could be taken in the streets,
from a bottle or a blunt. Or in a ring where
black fire's trained to rage,
fed with my own blood.

     Monster. *Rapist.* *Criminal.* *Gorilla.*

       Frankenstein.

          What did they expect?
Spoon out pain in 3-minute doses
for spit-dripping mouths always wanting—
then turn docile, meek, and "well-behaved,"
a grinning late-night talk show guest,
when the crowd goes home?   Fuck that.
What happens to a warrior when the war is done?

     I'm the necessary fallen angel you all
       wanted, the needed image
     flicker through your brain when you see
      some other Nigga on the street.

    You asked for The Perfect Fist.

      Here
      I Am.

Yona Harvey

In Toni Morrison's Head

White girls die first.
Which means I'm still
alive, but breathless and
on the run in the brain's
maze of scrutiny. How
I stumble in the memory
of Ohio, old names and faces
given me: Pecola, Dorcas,
Violet, Nel, First Corinthians.
Reinvention is my birthright.
With each step I am altered:
mother, daughter, river, sun. A tree
swells on my dark back
and no one waits in the future to
kiss me, only the towns-
women hissing at my
inappropriate dress, but not
at the sweet-talking rogue
who travels with me.
Inside the mire my heart
still pulses; at first, fatigued
and deathbound, then quick.
There's not enough milk
for all these babies or
the blue-eyed dolls yanking
their mouths open and shut.
Give a little clap, clap, clap,
chant the children and there's some-
thing ancient about the music's call
to order. *(Put them in your lap.)*
Who wouldn't stop to trace
the scars on the walls, their
embroidery of skin, stitches
that stretch for miles? *Not I,*
says the Jolly Old Woman
disappearing in a warm tunnel,
asking, *Toni, won't you tell me*

a funny story? I cut my losses
and sprint. I'm smoke, I'm ash,
Holy Ghost and Crucifix,
the preacher reborn to a body
in the grass, chirping, *Death
is so much different than I imagined.*

Terrance Hayes

Pine

I still had two friends, but they were trees.
—Larry Levis

In the dark we lugged someone's farfetched bounty
From a truck's black cab and it was a bad idea
And a bedevilment better than the rocks we'd thrown

At the dogs behind each low fence, the branches we'd torn
From saplings barely rooted to the fields, Boomie and I,
Our heads in a swivel of trouble, our two tongues

Swigging distractions, a few hours' worth of wrong turns
Behind us, we were restless and miles from home,
Dark boys roaming in the dark. We found a pickup truck

Unlocked outside a small hotel and in its cab: trash bags
Fat with clothing and housewares, a toaster and vacuum,
Waiting to be used again by someone checked in for the night,

Maybe a runaway wife reversing her dreams, a streak
Of red wine sleeping on her tongue while elsewhere
Her husband was in the dark because he didn't know yet:

She was gone, she was gone. For no good reason
We took the bags from the truck and propped them
Below the pine trees which, like everything in the dark,

Belonged to us. And to anyone approaching, our laughter
Must have sounded like the laughter of crows, those birds
That leave everything beneath them trampled and broken open,

Those birds dark enough to bury themselves in the dark.
But we were not crows, and we were not quiet until it was too late.
I was thrown against a tree as if I weighed less than a shadow,

A hand clutched the back of my neck as if it wasn't a neck.
Cuffed later inside the break-proof glass, I watched
The policemen nuzzling everything we'd touched,

Slithering, their faces calculating absolutes while the trash bags
Shimmered in a fiasco of light. When I looked up,
I saw Boomie nearly twenty feet high in the arms of a pine,

Almost nothing visible but his white shirt and white shorts.
I could feel him feeling as sorry for me as I felt for him,
And I said nothing. Think of what the tree might have said

If it could speak: *Hold me for a moment then, let me go . . .*
Something an unhappy housewife might say
To her husband on the last night of their marriage,

Or a boy to policemen when he's locked in a squad car.
I heard a voice between their voices issuing numbers,
Codes or uninterpretable verses, addresses in a bewildered city.

I was to be taken somewhere and given a name
More bona fide and afflicted, I was to be shot
Through the knee and then shot through the jaw,

Boomie must have thought. Even when the scene was clear,
He must have remained. It must have been like clinging
To the massive leg of God—

If the leg of God is covered in bark, if prayer is like waiting
For the darkness beneath you to change into something else,
If it's like waiting in the darkness to be changed.

Tonya Cherie Hegamin

Lovely's Song

Lovely's Song, Part 1

My name is Lovely
And I'm so pretty
My name is Lovely
And I am hot

All those bitches
They all just
Jealous
Cause they all know
That they are not

I hear them
Talkin
They all be sayin
My baby daddy
Is they baby daddy too

But all them chickens
They all just
Jealous
Cause they all know
That they are not

My name is Lovely
And I'm so
Pretty
My hair is long
And yours is not.

My man ain't
Creepin
We been together
For so many years.

All yall be
Hatin'
Stop spreadin rumors
Bout me and my
Pretty family.

All dose bitches
They all just wishin
They had my man
But they do not.

My name is Lovely
And I'm so pretty.
My name is Lovely
And I am hot.

Lovely's Song, Part 2

My name is   lovely
And I'm so   ugly
My name is   lovely
And I am   ugly

All those   girls
They all   up in my face

Cause they   want him
Well they   can have him

I hear them   whisperin

My baby daddy
Is they baby daddy   too?

All the   neighbors
They all be   knowin

They   hear me screamin
But they   don't call
                                                          the
                                                        police

My name is   ugly
And I'm so   ugly
My hair is   ugly
And   I can't make this stop

My man   fucks everybody
Creepin   even with little kids
We been   doin it
So many years   cause he make me

All yall be   turning backs to me
Stop spreadin   his seed
Rumors   are true   it's
Pretty   ugly

All them   should help   me
They just   watchin it
Wishin
They had   stopped it
When he   rape me
                         out in the street.

My name   is ugly
I am   only 14
My name   is stupid
And I   got a baby.

94

Sean Hill

Nigger Street 1937

McIntosh Street the sign reads
like the apple   red but not
red delicious red   but red
like redeye gravy on grits
at Gus's or red like stoplights
but they're also green and yellow
like apples in Allen's Market
on the corner   and red like
stoked coals   or embers   red
in Sol's forge   red   and red like
the stripe on Richard's barberpole
and the stitching around buttonholes
of overalls of those coming
to town on Saturdays and red
like the three ball   solid red
in the side pocket at the Blue Moon
and red like the eyes of those
late-staying patrons   early
in country churches on Sunday
mornings   and in church the red
of the edge of white pages
in a black bound bible
coming together   closing   red
as the congregation   rises.

Andre O. Hoilette

summer

I.

aunt sis is strong into her sixties
chickens in the red mud yard
come too close to her feed bucket
she seizes a brown hen's neck
whips the body around one handed
to close the windpipe

other times she would scatter grain
greedy hens come the closest

aunt sis throws the empty bucket
over the fat squatting body
drops her weight on it
hacks the neck with her cutlass
chicken body drums
inside the tin vessel
leaving the head
and eyes gasping for air

II.

hogs in summer
wait for their grassy shit to cool
then lie in it
doze in the corners
as rain strums octaves
on the zinc roof

she calls two men to the house
to help with the struggle
Sapoh and his brother
crest the hill and slide down
the gully path to bring up a hog

they return
Sapoh's broken smile
face black
sweaty like crude oil
rises over the hill
rope in hand
hog screaming
trotters stiff, stretched out like
an ironing board
his brother wrestling the hindquarters

III.

she only needs men to
tie the legs and hoist
the hog upside down to the hook
on the cement wall

aunt sis cuts the throat
all his will rushes at our feet
her cutlass slices the belly like a zipper
spills tripe and bowels
like curses, like obeah
into the killing pan

oily, visceral proteins smell the air
with the slaughtered swine

she quarters the animal
Sapoh hoses down the concrete
hog's spirit still floundering
suffocates in the congealing
masses of diluted blood

we don't see him transfigured
risen again
hogs stay dead
no enflamed phoenix soul
flies ahead to zion

Lita Hooper

Love Worn

In a tavern on the Southside of Chicago
a man sits with his wife. From their corner booth
each stares at strangers just beyond the other's shoulder,
nodding to the songs of their youth. Tonight they will not fight.

Thirty years of marriage sits between them
like a bomb. The woman shifts
then rubs her right wrist as the man recalls the day
when they sat on the porch of her parents' home.

Even then he could feel the absence of something
desired or planned. There was the smell
of a freshly tarred driveway, the slow heat,
him offering his future to folks he did not know.

And there was the blooming magnolia tree in the distance—
its oversized petals like those on the woman's dress,
making her belly even larger, her hands
disappearing into the folds.

When the last neighbor or friend leaves their booth
he stares at her hands, which are now closer to his,
remembers that there had always been some joy. Leaning
closer, he believes he can see their daughter in her eyes.

Erica Hunt

Poem for a Second

You have to live some
where and not
In the interrogative and
not in between   (not as a coefficient slang, salvage, drip)

You don't necessarily have to be
any where
any place
any time.

You only have
here   (rumpled rump, stubby toe cradled)
the some
where you live

To partition
your swallows
the bad from the
not so bad

After all
guilt is in the language
too good
to the last drop.

And ampersand   (with washed hands still)
gritty commas
sticky parens
get caught in the throat

You have to
English
the world to
become its possessor.

Become implicated in its
pretzel of ownership
of who owns   (in dual sense of the verb)
whom.

Sort it out
or become its
possession
a slave to others' thoughts.

You have to have
some place
where a thought gathers
critical mass   (dust)

Unabashed and disarmed
breaking down the coherent
limits of its
opposite frame of mind

To perfect
without caveat
some place to live
some where to go.

Kate Hymes

The Chosen One

> *Therefore I will give him a portion among the great . . .*
> *—Isaiah 53:12*

Mary sat on the back pew
among her brothers and sisters all
fresh from the cane fields
and long knives that cut down

strong, straight stalks that stood up
a head higher than the white boss man.
The pew, nothing more than rough
pine plank seats polished by butts wearing

Sunday best, sagged and swayed,
cradled Mary's expectant girth. The cardboard
Geddes funeral home fan slid down
the incline into her hopeful hand.

Mary waved the fan marking time
with the joyful noise. A flick of her wrist,
flap: "His eyes are on the sparrow
and I know he watches me." Flap, flap

through air pregnant with praise.
From the pulpit the clapboard prophet
delivered good words from the good book.
He preached Isaiah and called him Izear,

the way cane field folks said: *There will come*
a chosen one from among the oppressed
and afflicted. He will bring justice to the nations.
He will not be discouraged 'til he establishes justice on earth.

Then the preacher passed his best
handkerchief across his face to sop up hallelujah
sweat. Mary remembered the woman
who ran through the crowd to wipe the brow of

Jesus as he struggled with the cross.
If she could have run, she would have.
In her belly the baby jumped. She folded her hands
across her poked-out navel and prayed for a son.

Linda Susan Jackson

Family Outing

Because she was homesick for the smell
of Virginia tobacco and pit-roasted hog;
because she longed to hear her big brother
scratch out blues on his box; because
she craved the feel of corn silk
and had six stair-step children
before she was twenty-five,
she went to the funerals of strangers.

Twice a week, she'd dress up her five daughters
and the one son, fill a paper bag with saltines
smeared with peanut butter,
the oldest daughter, my mother,
carried, and out they'd go, roaming
the streets in search of a small cluster
of people, darkly dressed, and a hearse
in front of any building.

They grew as professional mourners,
learning funerals the way other children
learn the opera: funerals are opera—
grand affairs, perfumed buxom women,
stalwart-faced men and reserved seating
where they'd sit quietly, hands in laps,
crying on cue to *Precious Lord*
or any deep orchestral chord.

Major Jackson

from **Urban Renewal**

xvi: "What of my fourth grade teacher at Reynolds Elementary"

What of my fourth grade teacher at Reynolds Elementary,
who weary after failed attempts to set to memory
names strange and meaningless as grains of dirt around
the mouthless, mountain caves at Bahrain Karai:
Tarik, Shanequa, Amari, Aisha, nicknamed the entire class
after French painters whether boy or girl. Behold
the beginning of sentient formless life. And so,
my best friend Darnell became Marcel, and Tee-tee
was Braque, and Stacy James was Fragonard,
and I, Eduard Charlemont. The time has come to look
at these signs from other points of view. Days passed
in inactivity before I corrected her, for Eduard was
Austrian and painted the black chief in a palace in 1878
to the question whether intelligence exists. All of Europe
swooned to Venus of Willendorf. Outside her tongue,
yet of it, in textbooks Herodotus tells us of the legend
of Senwosret, Egyptian, colonizer of Greece,
founder of Athens. What's in a name? Sagas rise and
fall in the orbs of jumpropes, Hannibal grasps a Roman
monkeybar on history's rung, and the mighty heroes at recess
lay dead in woe on the imagined battlefields of Halo.

Honorée Fanonne Jeffers

Muse, a Lady Cautioning
for Billie Holiday

There's fairness in changing blood for septet's
guardian rhythm, the horn blossoming
into cadenza. No good pimp's scowl, his
baby's voice ruined sweet for the duration.

Yes, these predictable fifths. O, the blues
is all about slinging those low tales out
the back door (sing: child pried open on that
stained floor). O, Billie hollers way down dirt

roads (sing: woman on the verge of needled
logic). She's aware—yeah, I'm going to
kiss some man's sugared fist tonight. O, this
tableau's muse, a Lady cautioning me:

Just tough this thing out, girl. Sweat through the jones.
Don't ask for nothing. Spit your last damned note.

Tyehimba Jess

bud russel, louisiana prison transfer man, 1920

leadbelly you say.
killer   huh.
singer   huh.

look.

i herd them   gang by gang
moaning and dumb   cross country
to wherever   steel needs hands.
and there were   there are   so many—
enough to fill cotton fields   with hands.

you say he sang   played guitar.
seems like all of em   had a tune
buried under they breath   a itch
what ain't been   beat out of em
yet.
                  that is my work:
a kinda talent   to smell trouble
with a knife   and cut.

twelve-string   huh.
howler   huh.

let me tell you something.
they's all howlin'.
they a crop of twisted wind.
they was   they is   like   a harvest
i reap.

Amaud Jamaul Johnson

Spirit of the Dead Watching

> *Men are apt to idolize or fear that which they cannot understand,*
> *especially if it be a woman.*
>
> > —*Jean Toomer*

Like so many stones, a handful
of jasper or black opal scattered
along the banks of the Papenoo;

Gauguin has fixed his eye upon
a native girl working among the women.
She twists and beats the wash dry

for her mother, readying the bundles
to be carried back to their village,
and Gauguin is in love again.

Long from those indifferent hours,
long from the doors of the *Maison du jouir*
and the affected gaze of his mistresses.

In this paradise, all of his desires
collapse into color, become baskets
of guava, plantain, and avocado.

Tonight, he will offer her chocolate
and hold a red silk scarf before the fire.
Beneath banyan, palm, and sweet gum,

he will try to divine the body's secret,
unburden himself of the thought of history
and paint his language into their silences.

Brandon D. Johnson

listen

lust can beat men to mud. some learn
from calm women on cool sheets hard
as day-old grits.
she left a bathroom-wall message in rouge.
he won't touch his records, bluesmen
telling him what he couldn't hear before.
somewhere, lips print a cigarette, low tones chase
smoke from her mouth, crawl into the ear of another man.
now, he hears the sound of somebody else's arm
snaking round the waist of a red dress.

Karma Mayet Johnson

in the Quarter

pretty women with skirts that reach for their knees
twirl wickedly at the sky. cigar smoke teases rose-colored light.
duty soon will call us through her tropical hourglass, counting our names
like the grains of sand inside. for now, we'll breakfast on remoulade with violins,
our lips lush with lies and grenadine. let Paris kiss the feet of New Orleans.

doors creak open under water while birdsong pilfers your ear for a nest.
turning to this morning's third dawn, you mention a lover who complained
of your stingy kisses. be her, you ask. wail for my mouth til I beat you. then
you may suck my tongue. I had been frightened that first time. dildo snug,
lube in hand—I felt the amateur again, your voice spinning me invisible.

that afternoon I found you in Madrid—your blood wouldn't wait on nobody's siesta,
they'd better come out and sell you some pads—that afternoon I'd been ill-equipped.
it was orange leather then, not the strawberry suede cat-of-nine you lately prefer.
three of these months that yawn like plump kittens and I'm clutching for my sanity
the way you wrench the sheets when I'm precise.

machete is our music, pianissimo the cut. I sing into the dip between
shoulder and spine. elucidate the nape. how the belly infuses the barren palm.
hallow, hollow, shaved and slit. become my oven and terra cotta me
until we see the sun. fingers pruning what your suddenness has sown.
do not, do not loosen. do not bend.

I want to tell you something about myself, I admit between gasps,
and this I cannot say to a stranger. you twist the apricot of my upper thigh
by way of reply. the bruise will last for weeks. I knew I could not keep
a pact of anonymity. succumbing. you un-promise yourself as well.
Tequila, you are called. Tequila Brown.

A. Van Jordan

Kind of Blue

How I tried to explain
the love I heard between
the notes, how I reached
for you when he played,
how when a man's heart splits open
in the middle of a song—
whether playing or just connecting—
it is not unlike a gasp
for air, at the close of scx,
at that moment, how wondrous
our faces seem when we hear
a soul speak through a horn,
how perfect the grammar
between the notes.

And it was not because I knew
I would leave you years later,
in D.C.—once I found you
in bed with another man—
that I took you downtown
to see Miles Davis in concert
at Cincinnati's Music Hall;
it was just because you could leave me
and I knew—even then when I knew
nothing, when I had just bought
my first Miles Davis album—
I knew that good memories haunt us
as much as the bad ones.
And that night in '85
I think it was because I loved
him that you hated Miles Davis.
Oh, you wore that short skirt—
your legs pouring out
like two high Cs from a trumpet's bell—
but you still had an attitude.
You said he was a heroin addict,
a junkie, that his skin stretched

like leather because of drugs.
And I was reminded
of my neighbor who was on crack
and the night he came to beg for some money,
this guy who had a wife and two kids,
I asked him why he got high,
as if it were my business.
With his head turned from me he said,
Man, it's like you're havin' sex
and you come and you just keep
comin' and comin', 15 to 20 minutes straight
And then he looked at me and asked
Have you ever known love like that?
I gave him five dollars that night.

And despite your rolling eyes,
and the Tsssst you made with your teeth,
I bought you a ticket to the concert.
Remember how we sat on the front row
and how, in the middle of the first set,
Miles walked across the stage
on that tightrope invisible
to all but him, how he stepped at its edge,
and how he played "Time After Time"
and broke it down to you
and stared first at your legs,
and then straight into your eyes.
I wasn't jealous, you see,
because he made my point for me.
And to this day, because of that night,
I know for certain
that you still love one of us.
And look at you now, years later,
getting high in your apartment,
your stereo spinning a Miles Davis disc.
You no longer question
what kind of blue pulls a man's skin
so tightly over the face.
Yes. What do the uninitiated, who can only listen,
know about this kind of love?

Carolyn C. Joyner

The Now of Aunt Marie

Days of heat dissolve
in the cool damp of fall.
Walking alone, I know the time is now.
Now happens every year in October.

In the cool damp of fall,
now breaks the seal of memory's crowds.
Now happens every year in October,
slowly snaking the bends and turns of me.

Now breaks the seal of memory's crowds;
it freezes Aunt Marie in a final frame,
slowly snaking the bends and turns of me.
A shiver rushes through unsuspecting veins.

It freezes Aunt Marie in a final frame;
my walk becomes a run.
A shiver rushes through unsuspecting veins,
forced from a heart that knows all too well.

My walk becomes a run.
I want to leave behind the icy surge
forced from a heart that knows all too well,
in October when coral leaves wither and fall.

I want to leave behind the icy surge,
the cold I felt some twenty years ago
in October, when coral leaves wither and fall,
when Aunt Marie chose secretly to do the same.

It is the cold I felt some twenty years ago,
in autumn, when living things retreat to be reborn,
when Aunt Marie chose secretly to do the same,
to fly from a bridge, fall away like summer.

In autumn, when living things retreat to be reborn,
I see the fire of a dance fade to a flicker,
to fly from a bridge, fall away like summer,
whose days of heat dissolve.

John Keene

The Haymarket

no longer slings back rot-gut G&Ts before 2 A.M.,
as the doors close. These days, like the Napoleon,
Sporters, Bohemian, the Zone itself, it's a monument
to pure memory, but it already was dying
the evening we went to hear Jennifer Holiday
wail "And I'm Telling You," and jointly remarked how far
she'd fallen since the Kilimanjaro of *Dreamgirls*. Reconnecting
with her audience base is another way of putting it,
and she missed not a single note, hunched over that microphone,
song after song sweating through her spangles
like a dockworker, as men slid to and fro in shade
in front of the box stage. That was the night you tore
out my throat over my words with an ex, who you'd hurled
from your car years before when you first encountered
his tales of woe, whom later I observed sneak
out of Keller's to avoid a Brooklyn ass-whupping.
I wanted to remember that as the night two drag queens
tall as Masai threw down in front of the Dumpsters,
hurling pumps and wigs like gladiators, and a carnival-
sized crowd swelled the lot, pacing the glass, chatting,
cruising, watching the battle, as Warren offered play-by-play
(knowing the full tea) and Johnny offered up beauty
in a snaggled grin and slender Darrell, laughing, a cap
over his velvety brow, reintroduced himself to me,
who hadn't yet moved into love's house with you. But
that mêlée too occurred summers before, when that club
still felt new as a gift, alive, dangerous—though not as bad
as they'd warned us—and every man met I recalled
by name and face, half-believing I'd never see them again
because they'd disappear into wrong numbers conceived
on the spot, or ragged married lives, or the shadows
that only grew rattier in the club's corners when you drank
too much, or danced too much, or learned that someone else
you liked and hoped to hook up with had passed and you
stepped outside without a ride and missed the T knowing no taxis
were going to ferry you all the way back to Western Avenue
for less than $10, in that indifferent midnight Boston rain.

M. Nzadi Keita

soprano

woman unruffles crescendo
from a dark balcony
voice a wheelless chariot
aloose levitating
mid-height through summer
branches

whiskey in her treble some nights
moan making a slack belt
revival hymn to salt pork fingertips
nothing Sunday about that middle-range wanting
now she's running the scales again
like a girl with a secret

sometimes she handles the open cut
sometimes she stitches it up with palms
groping the note
sometimes she knots the thread of marvel
and lets it drop silver
from the metal rail

we lie in bed undone
dependent on
her tapestry to scrape the sheets
untie knuckles
and help us scratch out
urgent spells for the coming day

Ruth Ellen Kocher

Response to Pasiphae

Cousin, know about the white bull,
how your love for this creature
seized you,
your body captured.

But the alleyways,
the bus rides into the city, the cocks of men
you don't know. Did you finally
take him—cut thin lines, razored rows

plowed with a sippee straw cut in two,
or did it begin—veins opened to burden?
You, the beast in this story, mother
whose monster lives in my home,

child in Taurus who clamped
her teeth into my arm, beat my back, spit
her bad luck into my face—

Fathered by curses and left.
Fathered by a white desire,
vials, by a quarter-T,
a lighter, needle, spoon.

But she—the bull, also. A rack that carries you,
bliss I have stolen, a fix you've spent.
Tonight, she will collapse in my lap,
imagine the evening

a red flag, her small feet
hooved against earth.
She will close her eyes around fury,
charge towards the incarcerated heart of her sleep.

Yusef Komunyakaa

The Blue Hour

A procession begins in the blue—
        black gratitude between worlds,
& The Rebirth Jazz Band
        marches out of what little light
is left among the magnolia blooms.
        Step here, & one steps off
the edge of the world. Step there,
        & one enters the unholy hour
where one face bleeds into another
        as a horse-drawn buggy
rolls out of the last century,
        & the red-eyed seventeen-year locust
grows deeper into the old hushed soil.
        Lean this way, a blue insinuation
takes over the body. Step here,
        & one's shadow stops digging its grave
to gaze up at the evening star. Or,

at this moment, less than a half step
between day & night, birdhouses
stand like totems against the sky.

A flicker of wings & eyes,
mockingbirds arrive with stolen songs
& cries, their unspeakable lies & omens
as if they are some minor god's
only true instrument & broken way
on stage in the indigo air.

They come with *uh huh* & *yeah*,
a few human words, to ghost-white boxes
on twelve-foot poles,

to where each round door-hole
is a way in
& a way out of oblivion.

Jacqueline Jones LaMon

Clair de Lune

Mrs. Crowley plays the one song she says she knows.
It is almost *Clair de Lune,*
melody for a broken night, that no-good
moon hanging off to the side, hinged.
Her manicured pinky slipping to next, hitting
white instead of black, every time. She curses loud in thick
patois, then calls on Jesus, but no one looks away from the corpse

laid out in front of the rose settee. They all have come
to view him, his faded skin now clearly fallow, the yellow
moonlight bouncing through limbs of oaks at the curb,
through window-lace patterns of lilacs, falling
like ribbons of delicate candy, like tiny gold
coins on his cheeks. The mirrors, hard scrubbed

then shrouded for this round of neighborhood mourners—
the fine colored men holding last year's black fedoras,
the Democratic Club women in soft silk crepe de chine
with pressed and curled bobs under matching veiled hats,
making way from kitchen to parlor and back again, furrowed
in whisper, undoing his secrets, sending him home
for good. And soon, when the pots are washed of tender

meat and spicy roux, when the last clock is smashed,
his last used dish shattered and swept, then goes
Mrs. Crowley, guiding the widow, her hand: away from the body,
the moonlight, the marriage—up to the curve
of the second-floor stair, down the dark hallway,
cursing and fervent and leading the way.

Quraysh Ali Lansana

long way home
harriet

john   lord knows you still vexed   reckon me too if my wife stole
off durin sleepy night god an de devil only souls up at dat hour
even if i knows she bout to be sold south   even if i knows she
was leevin an you did   you so troubled when i talk bout leevin
call me a fool   call me cudjo   five years wid you john   yo wife
bout to be sold away   jus cus you free dis don't worry you none
you laugh   dunno if i'd miss yo laugh if i was in de south tho
thank ya jesus   gotta room in phildelphia john   aint big but clean
nuf room fo us   some chirren too   yo baby   i aint too old jus yet
jus round thirty-one   i think   make us a home john   one
where we's both free free from de lash's shadow   free like de lord
mean   got dis suit fo ya john   aint nobody worn dese clothes befo
walk proud in dese clothes   dese is free mans clothes

Carmelo Larose

The Sniff

My nine-year-old hand of bones bumped heads with my mother's
On a kitchen table full of chicken feet, kidney beans and brown rice.

In 1987 I wanted to disown my mother.
I rolled up my clothes in a bedspread and tied the sack to a twig
When she pulled out my favorite game,
Taunting me one last time with it.

Since we were only two we played the Draw Game, not Tiddly Wink,
Sebastopol, Bergen or Matador: games that required a full-blown
People: their liquor, their shouts, their prejudices.

My mother placed the twenty-eight dominoes pip face down
And shuffled the ivory backs with her pink- brown knuckles
Like a sorceress moving her hands over a cloudy crystal ball.

Then with the severity of knives we drew seven from the bone-yard,
The common pile of thick and heavy permutations of dice.
I went first and then later my mother even passed,

But I knew she had a plan: Caribbean home attendant wiping
A broken man's shit by day, she was a domino priestess at night.
Watch with all eyes those players of experience.

My mother had crossed the ocean and had even touched the back and fin
Of a shark. Once she let loose in my own room a bag of living, pinching
Blue crabs. When I ran under a table in fright, she laughed, saying
"Now you know what my childhood was like."

Before pearl of the Antilles, Haiti was now a stigma
Of the Atlantic. Land of independence and mountains, for years
The golden hills yielded hunger, indifference and more rock.
And in Brooklyn I caught fists for boat people, black spells and a virus.

I counted the pieces lying face up on the line and saw that my mother
Finally had to play a double, the sniff that opens up the game to four sides
Cross and endwise. My burdens would be lifted and I would run, the table,
My mother and my last name trembling in my wake.

But as she slammed the sniff down, and I claimed my first victory,
I realized what was just taught me: that to pick up the game,
Again and again is the only chance you have to relieve your hand of an inheritance of bones.

Virginia K. Lee

Yellow Is in the Eye of the Beholder
for Eartha Kitt

many of Eartha's own
do not believe
she's a *yella gal*
they don't know her hair
was a curly bush of rust red as a child

that in the chaos of her early years
her earth-colored mother
moss-brown baby half sister and she
begged door to door for food
in a small cotton town called North

her bed was often damp dirt
under a pine tree
in the forests of South Carolina
a blanket of leaves and
pine straw to keep warm

rocks of rejection
were thrown at her because
of the yellow tone of her skin
not high yellow
dark yellow
as in tiger
tiger eye
ripe corn
yam or
yellow envelope   pushed

when her mother
married a dark-skinned man
she was left behind with relatives

can't bring that yella gal to this marriage

still echoes
in the clash of voices
rumbling in her head

under teenagers' care
in the new family
she was
croaker sacked
tied to a tree
beat for fun
with peach tree switches
until she bled blue
and lost her tears

they parted her legs
probed violated
robbed her of childhood innocence
until she fractured into five puzzled selves

> *Ear tha Ma e   the child*
> > *the Zombie   numbed from wounds of hurt*
> > > *the Sub-conscious D evil   who   creates fear   and   sickness*
> > > *Spirit Mother who watches her from above* and
> *Eartha Kitt   dancer   singer   actor*

who emerged from the red dust
to find the long winding
yellow clay road to fame
but not freedom
from jaundiced color-struck demons

Raina J. León

Christ and Magdalene

for Rich "El Profe" Villar

Saliva-slick finger rested forgotten on my knee
pages would not turn alone
he read heavy words to leap into my loom
weave a piece of him
to wuther is to put one's hand under glass in noonday sun
flesh burn to bone for hours
how he loved me
how he pushed heaven heights until
       "the rainy night had ushered in a misty morning"

time was time, stealing mechanic joints still vibrating
to fill dusty clothes from lovers
long gone and never coming back
we tussled salt lost to powdery clean
I gave him my quiver, he gave his open mouth in moans
prayers to his father in the other room
humming a respirator song
       "I put slight faith in his own affirmation"
a man is as constant as the devil on holiday

return is a promise
to lose himself again in tangles
my hair the only bondage he ever loved
frizzed dry, rough, bed-misshapen
he kissed thick strands, called them silk
closed my eyes with his lips he left me
with no picture of him
       "temporary brooks crossed our path"

if sorrow has a name I would take it on
cut his voice from my ear
like Bedouin women hack hair in mourning
rub my body in red
coral to make skin break for rivers
cloak the scars in burlap and itch
       "my feet were thoroughly wetted"
his cleansed by desert sand

"I was cross and low"
I'll be the cross lowered
if he is where I land

Quotations are from *Wuthering Heights*.

Doughtry "Doc" Long

The Devil Is Beating His Wife Again

strange sight
sun on one side of the street
rain on the other
steam rising from the pavement like hell
flowers pretending not to notice
when it rains like this
it means the devil is beating his wife
something she has done did not please him

but if he and his wife suppose to be so bad
and study only the evil and negative
why is he beating her
what did she do
she couldn't have done something wrong
because wrong is bad, and that's
right down the devil's alley

so she must have done something good
to have pissed him off, maybe she
was caught in bed with thoughts
of slow dancing and barbecued ribs
bought roses, smiled back at a glass of wine or
told him she loved him
or caught a life-affirming glance
while passing a mirror

something went wrong
to have made him go off
to have provoked this sudden
downpour this deluge
sun's out, and it's raining like nobody's business

devil chasing his wife
down the street with a stick
she trying to run with only one shoe on
people in the neighborhood shouting
ducking, rushing for cover

Kenyetta Lovings

Artificial Insemination of a Working-Class Lesbian

There are runny things on the kitchen sink tear-warm to touch. Her arms are splayed, held out from her body on the counter top. While a syringe, long and tubular, meets a helmet of night inside her, her knees bewitch the sky. A fly swims circles in the air, and plants its body full of eggs on a plastic paisley cup. The day breaks through dusty glass, through aloe and snake plants like backlit gauze. Reluctant yellow light ties her fawn-colored lips shut. Behind resplendent flesh her teeth are clenched, her jaw is lantern. A crest of her wiry hair blankets embryonic gardens. These are enclosures of wild hyacinth and hibiscus tides over the edge of precipice.

Adrian Matejka

Understanding Al Green

When I was twelve, a wiser sixteen-
year-old told me: *If you really want
to get that, homeboy, you best be bringing
Al Green's Greatest Hits. And if you ain't
in the mix by song five, either she's
dyking it or you need to re-evaluate your
sexual orientation. Know what I'm saying?*

With those words, I was off—borrowed Al
Green in the clutch in search of that *thing*.
Socks pulled up to my neck. A curl. Real
tight Hoyas jersey was nothing but regulation
and I knew I was smooth and I knew
I was going to be in the mix by song five.
The whole walk from the ball court,

the wise man's words echoed like somebody's
mama banging on the door: *The panties
just be slippin' off when the women hear
Al's voice. Slippin'.* Slippin' because Al
hits notes mellow, like the silk that silk
wears. His voice is all hardworking nighttime
things. Not fake breasts, but you

and your woman, squeezed onto the couch,
taking a nap while the aquarium stutters
beside you. Nodding off on drizzly days
when you should be at work. The first
smoke after a glass of fine wine you know
you can't afford. Nobody, woman
or man, knows how to handle Al Green.

That Girl from Ipanema would have
dug Al. Her panties, flip-flopping right
there by the sea. That sexy passing
the Pharcyde by would have stopped to say
What up? if they were Al. But they weren't.
And neither were you, last night when
that woman at the club shut you down:

I got a man . . . blah, blah, blah. Hate to tell you,
player, but she's at Al's place right now asking
for an autograph and maybe a little sumpin-
sumpin. What is sumpin-sumpin? I don't know.
But Al knows. And I'm sure you've heard that old
jive about Al getting scalding grits thrown on him.
You have to recognize those lies because

he would have started singing and those grits
would have been in the mix, too. For real.
I never believed the pimp-to-preacher story
anyway. The point is, Al's voice is like G-strings
and afro wigs and trying to be quiet when
the parents are home. The point is Al Green
hums better than most people dream.

Shara McCallum

An Offering

I am the woman at the water's edge,
offering you oranges for the peeling,
knife glistening in the sun.
This is the scent and taste
of my skin: citron and sweet.
Touch me and your life will unfold
before you, easily as this skirt
billows then sinks,
lapping against my legs, my toes
filtering through the river's silt.
Following the current out to sea,
I am the kind of woman
who will come back to haunt
your dreams, move through you
humid nights the way honey
swirls through a cup of hot tea.

Carrie Allen McCray

The First Time We Heard "Flyin' Home"
tribute to Lionel Hampton on learning of his death—2002

(*early 1940s*)
Lionel Hampton
    "Flyin' Home,"
    riffin' on his
vibraphone,
    out in the hall
neighbors meet
    movin' to the beat
on the radio

    Groovin' hips,
tappin' feet

    someone hollerin',

    "Yeah, aw reet"
faster, faster
    oh, how sweet
    shakin' off a
    hard-time week
    in Harlem
        one Saturday mornin'

Ernesto Mercer

One More Silver Dollar: (The Midnight Rider Turns)

Another ghetto room, same old
duffel of songs flitting the arc
of another bare bulb. I know
the lyrics without listening anymore.
I know the words under
the words, the words beneath
the instrumentals & now I know
saxophone solo, six bent strings or
blue bruised throat—they're all
the same song, we all know by heart—
those of us who never learned
or learned too dearly, too much
always just passing through,
taking the names we're given
without complaint—we know
each other by reading our
scarifications. Hats low
ride our eyes, protection against
the glare of burning bridges.
We never sit with backs to doors
& blueprint the fire exits on entry,
knowing six-day saints worship
Satan come Saturday night
& any moment may erupt
when both Jokers are shuffled
in the deck. We keep our bags
close, the first thing smoking on
our minds. Bottles, pipes
& needles erode the years;
but neither the hustlers nor
the pharmacists peddle the elixir
that banishes the Wolf, the Butcher,
the Posse—the **whatever** we
know is three steps behind.
We mostly see our faces floating
above the broken lines of midnight
turnpikes, everything we know

about this life, America,
ourselves, stenciled on our pulses,
drumming us, to one more
cheap room. Thing is, I
remember the boy who wanted
the world so bad, the boy with wings
on his ankles desperate for
the breakaway velocity
to get there. Lately it's just
been about speed. I don't know
that I could tell you anymore
when it all came down
to *they'll never take me alive.*
Now, I'm not even sure I
remember who **they** are at all;
but the music, the blood, the feet
all hum: *get away.* Three things
I know for sure: there's a bush
of spirits darker than Mississippi
midnight just beyond the shoulder
of the mind's bright expressway;
the Soul is a long graffiti wall
none of us will ever decipher
clear enough to read; & a brotha's
heart is the strangest gris-gris
parlour—four chambers full
of stuff you've only heard
tell of, but never knew
you'd need. I don't dream
of winged ankles anymore. I
want some ground to stand on.
Whoever you are behind me,
whatever it is you got—Ace
of Spades, cleaver, or shiny mirror—
here I am:

                    Ernesto,
Babyboy from old Que Street,
& here is all I have—heart & balls
swinging naked between the skins
of the old, old songs, throat exposed
& open *santo vocce vibrato*
with this strange new won note.

Dante Micheaux

The Temple of Greed & Mildew

after Yusef Komunyakaa

There is a casino on the other side of town
that can offer you a good time
until you run out of money.

People do the damnedest things
after giving that last chip to the roulette table:
a man takes out his eyes & uses them as dice;
a woman loses her rent money playing poker
& sits on the floor pulling out her hair
one strand at a time,
trying to weave it into the carpet
with a piece of fingernail.

It is impossible to leave with any winnings.
A statue of a satyr, by the door,
picks your pockets as you leave.

Jonathan Moody

Relapse of Winter in Frankfurt

I don't want to do it again,
I can hardly bear to look
at her—Beth, my babysitter,
sixteen or so, who covers
my skittish body with kisses.
A song that resembles
Rachmaninov's "Prelude
in C Sharp Minor" plays
behind the frigidity
of cream curtains. It's
mid-March. Empty
Heinekens all but blanket
the bedroom floor. Right
now I could be skating
to the corner market
for butterscotch. But Beth
is on her back cramming
my hand down cropped
denims. Her left leg,
a pine cone pendulum
knocking against the vanity.

Kamilah Aisha Moon

What a Snakehead Discovered in a Maryland Pond and a Poet in Corporate America Have in Common

> *The snakehead is a voracious fish from China's Yangtze River. It can breathe air and "walk" on land—able to crawl out of the water and survive for up to three days while searching for a new body of water if necessary. These critters could devastate the native ecosystem and be almost impossible to control.*
>
> —James A. Swan, "Snakehead Sightings"

My fins are foreign, my gills versatile
because they've always had to be.
Despite alleged aggression,
I cut these teeth for protection.

You understand how the others swim,
but me—my travel mystifies,
terrifies a little.
You figure if you don't "get" me,
I'll somehow get you good—
invading and transforming the habitat forever.

How do you do what you do?
Where are you coming from?
How should I manage you?

I propelled myself upon rugged land
to reach this pond,
buried in the muddy bottom for years.
Both of us marvel
that I've survived this long undetected.

Keep your poisons, your devious nets,
whatever ridding you have in mind.
There is no need to slice and bleed me.
Just because I can doesn't mean I ever planned
to wipe you out.

I've heaved my greatness before.
I'll do it again,
back to incredible, exotic waters in which
you would drown.

Indigo Moor

Tap-Root

i

Concrete drew the M'ssippi back like a fist.
The river buried itself and waited out
plow blades swinging through dry harvest.
Rough-handled hoes turning soil
hard enough to raise the Blues.

ii

Muddy Waters sprang whole, dry-
heaved from the knotted center
of a plank-wood shack.
Shook hisself loose of blood,
dirt, moonshine, the ass-dark end
of a mule and was gone.

iii

Since, twisters have spun the shack
'round, bent its insides out, 'til it
vomited its secrets on boot-dust road.
Now tourists use splintered slivers
of history as toothpicks.

iv

A little ways down the road
you can squander a week's pay,
sleep in an old slave shack.
Spend a day picking cotton.
Smile for pictures.

v

The M'ssippi used to cover
these parts, until they dammed

it up, held its tongue like words
you choke back in church
to keep your insides from escaping.

vi

Staring across dusty fields
you can ache the need for river.
Almost drown in longing for water
that won't come here no more.

Lenard D. Moore

A Quiet Rhythm of Sleep

March midnight creeps upstairs
while my wife and daughter sleep
on the new brass bed that darkness blankets
as a hard wind rattles the panes
and thunder booms like artillery rounds
blasting the vast night.

I sit downstairs writing about night
while slight snoring scatters upstairs
as the TV talks of exploding rounds
like those that shattered my father's sleep
in a building with shivering panes
on a green cot without blankets.

In the jungle no one needed blankets.
Terror must have gnawed bones at night
like rigid wind splinters panes
and infinite chill climbs stairs.
No matter how hard I try I can't find sleep
while late-night TV resonates rounds.

I imagine how my father ducked rounds
beneath a sky like heavy blankets
that smothered soldiers in sleep
and snuffed out lifelong dreams of night.
I pray to the Man Upstairs
to rid that charred land of constant pains.

With pen I tap sturdy brilliant panes
in this house of memory where rounds
are falling like rain; here it is safe upstairs:
my woman and child rest beneath blankets,
their chests lift and fall with night
in a quiet rhythm of sleep.

I wish my father might fathom such sleep
without the rattling of cracking panes

in the dubious, dwindling night,
without patrolling like a guard making rounds
but wear his nights beneath blankets
as peace settles like dust-motes upstairs.

My wife and daughter sleep without dreaming panes
and rounds shaking away the inkblack night.
I imagine my father walking upstairs, blinking at blankets.

Harryette Mullen

Drinking Mojitos in Cuba Libre

"My mojito in La Bodeguita. My daiquiri in El Floridita." A postcard of fidelity shaking hands with earnest money. Lost in the streets of Havana, gasping for breath *como un pez sin agua*. As hot as it is, as black as can be, as dark as this combustible star. *Sí, hace calor, pero* only *turistas* wear big brims or ultraviolet lenses. You hot? You thirsty? You buy us mojitos? You bring your *yanqui dolor.* We show our splendid squalor. Milk for baby, you give me dollar. You black, we black. See my scar from the war in Angola. Still working for a *Cuba libre.* Tropicola's sweeter than Coke. Mix rum and sugar with sweat of a slave. We work for pesos and beg for your stinking dollar. I'll show you where Hemingway wrote, the bar where he sipped his swizzle. You'll owe me a mojito. *Que se vayan los gusanos.* Crush with a pestle. Add rumba. Stir briskly with a drop of African blood.

Marilyn Nelson

Woman with a Chignon

Picasso

Her jaundiced face and habitual half sneer
turn toward you level, disappointed eyes.
You make her want to spit: youth, hope, desire:
soon enough, life will knock you to your knees.
What she could tell you about how love dies.
But would you believe a truth that came from her?
Or would you think her capable only of lies
because her hands are rough from scrubbing floors?
At a table set for one in a café
she sips gin-flavored, slowly melting ice,
swallowing the sad stories she could tell.
You wouldn't want to hear them, anyway.
You're much too you, too much in love, too nice.
Her eyes slide past you, damning you to hell.

Mendi Lewis Obadike

In The Way That Longing Is, a sonnet cento for Cave Canem

this space in me that was seriously emptied

that ties this section together for me

you open your mouth to speak an

there is this interruption. of, you could say, space

another kind of sense other than the story

speed and style. in that puzzling thing

your new thang. Still wound up b

the different ways we can respond to one anoth

Somewhere in me I know that i

poetry that feeds me. I want a name for i

for those strange, unarticulated questio

right beyond my gras

i want more of that but can't get it. that poem

painful, in some inexplicable w

The sonnet cento is a form I invented for myself in order to address my questions about poetry as a form of communication. When I write a poem, so much of what I write comes from conversations I have had with other writers about big concepts, small words, and what we want from poetry itself. In the sonnet cento, the language of the

Dear Dear, what is this about? i want to know and don't want to know.
do you imagine that there is also such a thing as an UNwilling reader?
Why "my mother" in place of "mummy"? you all filled up
                                        inside my head
i had everybody. And i can tell you that "sun" is a word
                            more than "shoes." sun? i think
it's what the sun is, as heat and light. but it was like that feeling when
                            nothing comes out. the spaces not
filled there are like that open. the part of the mouth that gapes.
                            but not silence. a filling
up of something that disrupts the narrative. not an abstraction, in that
sense of a sliver of a bigger thing. but an imposition of
                            the act of listening comes
o the front. lenard and i had some interesting conversations about
                            the attention of the
writer to the reader. hey, i'm talking to you. I cannot wait to read
                    Annotations. i feel as if i'm
peaking too much about this small part. it made me think about all
                            as artists. "just" is
nother word at work. "They are just shoes." I have been calling it fear
of not being a poet, but I think it's just longing to be heard.
                            not the word, it's the knowledge. I
mean, the experience of having traipsed through the stuff they call
                            beautiful, in a sad way.
Could there be a title that directed us somewhere else? and thanks
                            about blackness that got
nswered for me. reading your work is a kind of reaching. something
                    and sometimes i touch it. sometimes i don't.
ometimes i touch it and want to grab my hand back, wipe it off. how
o you say that in English? it was painful in the way that longing is.
                            back on the
rawing board. i enjoyed reading your long letter. but it was kind of
                    perfect timing, yes? thanks for
aying that. i feel completely drained. the desire to know more

poem is literally taken from my letters to other writers. In the case of this poem
those writers are Cave Canem poets Ronaldo V. Wilson, Christian Campbell, Dawn
Lundy Martin, and John Keene. The poem itself is in the language lifted from the
conversations, but it is also in the empty spaces forged by those conversations.

Gregory Pardlo

Winter After the Strike

You believe,
if you cast wide enough

your net of want and will, something meaningful
will respond. Perhaps we are the response—

each a cresting echo hesitating, vibrant with the moment
before rippling back.

But you're steadfast as Odysseus strapped to the mast, as you were
in '81 when Reagan ordered you back to work. You were president

of the union local you steered with your workingman's voice,
the voice that ground the Ptolemaic ballet of air-traffic to a temporary stop.

You used it to refuse to cross the picket line I walked
with you outside Newark International.

I miss sitting beside you at the console when you worked
graveyard shift in the tower. Mom and I visited with our sleeping bags.

I could see the dark Turnpike for miles, the somber
office buildings winking insomniac cells, the tarmac

spread before us like a picnic blanket and you, like a jade Buddha
suffused in the glow of that radial EKG.

You'd push the microphone in front of me, nod, and let me give the word.
I called all my stars home, trajectories bent on the weight of my voice.

You say you miss tracking those leviathans, each one snagged on the barb
of your liturgy. I too get reeled in by the hard, now rusty music of your pipes.

I follow it back to the day of your accident in the story you tell:
you were sixteen, hurdling the railings dividing row house porches

from one end of Widener Place to the other to impress Mom.
I imagine the way you cleared each one like a leaf bobbing on water, catching

the penultimate, the rubber toe of your Chuck Taylors kissed
by the rail, upsetting your rhythm, and you roiled in the air headlong,

arms outstretched, stumbling toward the last like one hell-bent
or sick to the stomach. The way you landed, on your throat, the rail

could have taken your head clean off. Since then, your voice issues
like some wartime communiqué: a ragged, type-written dispatch

which you swallow with your smoker's cough black as a tire
spinning in the snow. That winter after the strike,

we were so poor you sold everything but the house. Tell me, Dad,
when you'd stand at the door calling me in for the night,

could you hear me speaking to snowflakes falling beneath the lamppost?
Could you hear me out there, imitating you imitating prayer?

Carlo Toli Paul

The only shine on the Titanic
for Joseph Phillipe Lemercier Laroche and his descendents

3:18 P.M.; Thursday, April 11, 1912

Did you know that you're the only "shine" on the Titanic?
Seems to be the standard icebreaker, dear Uncle.
Now, from a bespectacled Brit
whilst making his rounds on deck.
Once again
I must glaze over the swift miscalculation.
Despite my girls' even complexion
we are indeed, a total of three Negroes aboard.

7:56 P.M.; Friday, April 12, 1912

If I wanted to explain
how far I have come
repeat myself
and my credentials
every day
as if I were back in engineering class
I would have stayed in France.
How do I say this
to my wife?
She does not understand . . .

10:04 A.M.; Saturday, April 13, 1912

This ship is quite striking.
Upper deck.
Lower deck.
The cigar room.
Saloon.
Chandeliers.
Oak paneling.
Palm courts.
Silk curtains.
Musical ensembles.

After four days at sea
it is still impossible for us to get around
all the stares.

1:26 P.M.; Sunday, April 14, 1912

Had an interesting conversation with a crew member.
He asked me which coast of Africa Haiti sits on.
I told him Haiti is an independent nation on the Atlantic
where you currently preside and showed him your picture.
Uncle, he laughed at the idea of a Negro president.
But asked me not to take offense. He said he also laughed
when he heard that a Colored was on board.
Apparently, this is a White Star Line first.
I told him how Haiti became the first independent Negro nation
in 1804. He shrugged and over his shoulder
he reminded me that I boarded second class.

2:31 A.M.; Monday, April 15, 1912

I am thinking of you, Uncle,
and the safety of my wife and girls.
It was unthinkable to watch
that full, white ship
disappear
into empty darkness
so smoothly, shrink
to an afterthought
of ocean waves.

I hope my reflections find you

this
freezing water
pulls
like rope
around
my legs, arms, neck.

The only shine on the Titanic
is all I think about.
It echoes in my mind, in the waves.

And this is not right
that my tragedy
is unremarkable.

If I am the only shine,
Uncle, why
is death déjà vu?
And why do I see myself
drowning
in this Atlantic
over and over
again?

Gwen Triay Samuels

Ode to the Triays of Amelia

I will die on Amelia,
the Isle of May.
It will be on a Wednesday
to give all my kinfolks enough time
to fly home from everywhere
for a Saturday funeral.

The kids will argue
about cremating me
then they'll remember I
told them there is no room
on the Black Catholic side
of Bosque Bello cemetery
which means "beautiful forest"
where the back-door Triays
are buried, sons and daughters
of Spaniards and ex-slaves.

They will finally cremate me
and scatter my ashes
all over Old Town,
once entirely owned by
my Free Mulatto Triay grandfathers
who built the seawall on top of
Seminole bones and
who birthed the shrimping industry,
even though the Greeks and Italians
got all the credit.

They will scatter me some more
over what developers left unruined
of American Beach,
which we used to call
"the Black Beach" where
they made us go because they
didn't think we were American,
but where we were glad to go

because A. L. Lewis
made it our own.

Then they will scatter me
on "Amelia Island Plantation"
the rich white folks' resort
built by developers
on the tombstones and homesites
of a desecrated Gullah-Geechee village.

I will not let them forget
"Historic Downtown Fernandina"
where they will rub some of my ashes
over the word "Traeye"
on the first British census
to anglicize my name.

Finally, they will scatter me
on the corner of Estrada Street
which means "to stride"
and Ladies Street
which was "Calle de las Damas"
where African and Mulatta whores
serviced the seafaring men and
offered low-rate placage
to nearby conquistadores.

And then, in due time, my ashes
will rise up in stride
quick-like into a storm
that will blow over
all of Amelia
and claim her once again as mine.

The Triays of Amelia Island are the African American descendants of the slave-holding Triays of Saint Augustine, one of the Spanish (Menorcan) families who founded the city. Amelia is a barrier island off the coast of northeast Florida, some forty miles north of Saint Augustine, where the slave masters purchased land for their free mulatto offspring. Amelia shares a history similar to those of Hilton Head, Saint Helena's, and other U.S. barrier islands. The Old Town section of Fernandina Beach, Amelia's main city, was platted before Saint Augustine and rightfully claims the title of "Oldest City in the United States."

Sonia Sanchez

Under a Soprano Sky

I.

once i lived on pillars in a green house
boarded by lilacs that rocked voices into weeds.
i bled an owl's blood
shredding the grass until i
rocked in a choir of worms.
obscene with hands, i wooed the world
with thumbs

while yo-yos hummed.
was it an unborn lacquer I peeled?
the woods, tall as waves, sang in mixed
tongues that loosened the scalp
and my bones wrapped in white dust
returned to echo in my thighs.

i heard a pulse wandering somewhere
on vague embankments.
O are my hands breathing? I cannot smell the nerves.
i saw the sun
ripening green stones for fields.
O have my eyes run down? i cannot taste my birth.

2.

now as i move, mouth quivering with silks,
my skin runs soft with eyes.
descending into my legs, i follow obscure birds
purchasing orthopedic wings.
the air is late this summer.

i peel the spine and flood
the earth with adolescence.
O who will pump these breasts? I cannot waltz my tongue.

under a soprano sky, a woman sings.
lovely as chandeliers.

Tim Seibles

Ambition: II. Mosquito in the Mist

You human-types, you
two-legged sapien-sapiens,
you guys are walkin' smoothies
ta me, milkshakes wearin' trousers,
a cup'a coffee mowin' a lawn.

I gotta hand it to you though—
all the colors, the smells, tall,
petite, skinny-minnies or whoppin'
whale-sized motha'humphries—you
got variety: I'm zippin' around
some summa' nights and it's like
an all-you-can-eat situation.

And I like the threads—hiphop
baggies, halter tops, baseball caps,
culottes—stylin'! And
most'a the fabric's flexible enough
for me and my little straw.

But I sense some chronic
unfriendliness, some ongoing
agitation from you hemaglobes.
My family and me are small things
tryin'a quench a thirst. It's our nature.

The random violence is really
uncalled for. The bashing, the swatting . . .
And *the cursing*! Fuck you guys, man!
It's like you never heard'a the word
compromise.

And the worst
is when you bring down the curtain
right in the middle
of a good suck. I don't think
I need ta spotlight the obvious

analogy, but ok: imagine yourself
alone wit' someone you want

real bad—*her skin is toffee,*
his hair is an avalanche
of dreadlocks—and
the moment
comes: the shared
shimmer in the eyes and you
lean into the kiss, warm
and rich as God's
good cocoa, your mouth's
famished apparatus
slurping up the sweetness,

when—as if from hell's
rabid handbag—a smack,
big as Godzilla, knocks the livin'
juji-fruit outta you.

The luscious touches, the hum
of two hearts, the holy
communion flung into the fat-ass dark forever.
What? You think we ain't
got feelings!? I got the memories.
It's all in the genes! See,
you big-holes-in-the-face motha'humphries
don't never think nothin'
about other kinds'a life,

but that's ah'ight, I got dreams. I got
big plans. I'm all itchy and bumpy
wit' discontent—and you might not
see it, but I'm gettin' bigger—I
been liftin'—and someday I'm gonna
get a little payback on the go:

land on your cheek like a
round-house kick, and before
you can pick up your nostrils
I'm gonna drink you dry, drain ya
to the lees—you'll be

layin' there stiff as beef jerky,
your arrogant balloon
all flat and wrinkly while I
lift off like a, like a

helicopter, like a goddam
12-cylinda' angel, like a bulldozer
wit'a probiskamus big
as a' elephant's dick.

Elaine Shelly

W. E. B. in Ghana

I've been dancing so fast
between philosopher and threat
I've forgotten on which side
of the dance floor I stand
Should I waltz or shake
my hips in a fast huckabuck
Is it minuet or juicy grind
And how long can I ask
these questions

Cherene Sherrard

Parade of Flesh

1.

A bowl of green tamarinds
balances, despite the rocking
of the punt.

Water dissembles,
I hold my parasol low—
all that is visible
to spectators picnicking
in the *bois du bologne*
is a sliver of shoulder
pale against dark waves
of hair.

We make a modern tableau:
he, cravat askew, shirt sleeves
rolled back display athletic forearms.
I reach for a single tamarind
clasp my sunshade to my chest
peel the skin with my teeth.

2.

The crowd, a swath of Paris
powdered dignitaries, fops holding
skirts aside from the unwashed rabble.
For a franc, every stratum can view
the exhibition of the latest hottentot.
One would presume that Robespierre still
reigned over the *tricolore*, the fever for blood
hot under the skins of all good *citoyens*.
Intrigued always by the decadent,
Charles procured tickets for us both.
He gestures to the raised wooden platform,
compares my diluted charms with her fecundity.
If I lower my veil no one can see the tears

coursing the powdered chalk. We press inward.
Afraid to meet her eyes I focus on the spot
just below her torso, before the flesh rounds
above her pubis. I recognize her resignation,
the acknowledgment that they rejoice
to see hands stretch over the parts you wish
to hide and feed on your shame at having
too few digits. I am proud to see she makes
no attempt to cover herself from grasping eyes.
The crowd pushes us closer to the platform,
I lose hold of my purse. Charles ducks to catch it.
I am surprised to see "ladies" mixing with commoners—
no one is too refined for this sort of entertainment.
As we retreat, those who cannot see riot. From her view,
the onlookers figure an undulating maelstrom.
Her skin takes on the greenish cast of a changeling,
the color does not detract; black skin, the audience
thinks, does not reflect anything.

3.

As the rose-gilded morning creeps
across the esplanade, stains
the *Sacré Coeur*, I sweep dead leaves
from the iron chairs on our balcony
sit wrapped in his *manteau* to watch
the clouds chase the sun. The city
is quiet, night's astringent renders
human stench odorless. Soon,
the *boulangerie* beneath us
will throw open its shutters.
Claudine, the baker's daughter,
will leave a basket of breads
outside our door and I will
return it with roses, cut in
adolescence from our garden cloister.
It is a fair exchange. This life.

Kevin Simmonds

The Poet, 1955

After poor Emmett Till,
he wrote a poem to work out his faith
in things unseen.

We'd all seen too much:
Emmett's waterlogged face, the teenage in him
snatched by his opened mouth to a dog of a woman;

a mother seeing what the South
had conjured for her son,
and the radiance of her voice in front of the cameras,

rising
through the falling
of her son.

Sunday following,
Reverend had him recite.
He called Emmett Till a mansion,

a mansion of a boy
whose rooms we
must fill.

Patricia Smith

Asking for a Heart Attack

for Aretha Franklin

Aretha. Deep butter dipt, scorched pot liquor, lick
off the sugarcane. Vaselined knock-knees clacking
weird gospel, waddling south, the direction of our
mother's land. Miss 'retha. Greased, glowing 'neath
limelight, sanctified moan its own defense, turning
ample ass toward the midnight hour. The goddess
of steamed cornbread and bumped buttermilk know
Jesus by His *first* name. She was the one sang His
drooping down from that ragged wooden T, dressed
Him in blood red and shine, conked that holy head,
rustled up bus fare and took the Deity downtown.
They found a neon backslap, coaxed the DJ, slid
electric till the lights slammed on. *Hey, don't know
where you goin', but you can't stay here.* She taught
Him dirty words for His daddy's handiwork, laughed
as he first sniffed whiskey's surface, groaned as He
touched His hand to what was blue in her. She was
young then, spindly and ribs paining, her heartbox
suspicious of its key. So Jesus blessed her, opened
her throat and taught her to wail that way she do,
she do wail that way don't she do that wail the way
she do wail that way, don't she? Now when 'retha's
fleeing screech reach been-done-wrong bone, all the
Holy Ghost can do is stand at a respectable distance
and applaud. And maybe shield His heart a little.
So you question her several shoulders, the soft stairs
of flesh leading to her chins, the steel bones of an
impossible dress biting into bubbling obliques?
Ain't your mama never told you how black women
collect the world, build other bodies onto their own?
No earthly man knows the solution to our hips,
asses urgent as sirens, titties Xed with pulled roads.
Ask us why we pray with our dancin' shoes on, why
we grow fat away from everyone and toward each other.

Tracy K. Smith

Duende

1.

The earth is dry and they live wanting.
Each with a small reservoir
Of furious music heavy in the throat.
They drag it out and with nails in their feet
Coax the night into being. Brief believing.
A skirt shimmering with sequins and lies.
And in this night that is not night,
Each word is a wish, each phrase
A shape their bodies ache to fill—

> *I'm going to braid my hair*
> *Braid many colors into my hair*
>   *I'll put a long braid in my hair*
> *And write your name there*

They defy gravity to feel tugged back.
The clatter, the mad slap of landing.

2.

And not just them. Not just
The ramshackle family, the *tios*,
Primitos, not just the *bailaor*
Whose heels have notched
And hammered time
So the hours flow in place
Like a tin river, marking
Only what once was.
Not just the voices scraping
Against the river, nor the hands
Nudging them farther, fingers
Like blind birds, palms empty,
Echoing. Not just the women
With sober faces and flowers
In their hair, the ones who dance
As though they're burying

Memory—one last time—
Beneath them.
                    And I hate to do it here.
To set myself heavily beside them.
Not now that they've proven
The body a myth, parable
For what not even language
Moves quickly enough to name.
If I call it pain, and try to touch it
With my hands, my own life,
It lies still and the music thins,
A pulse felt for through garments.
If I lean into the desire it starts from—
If I lean unbuttoned into the blow
Of loss after loss, love tossed
Into the ecstatic void—
It carries me with it farther,
To chords that stretch and bend
Like light through colored glass.
But it races on, toward shadows
Where the world I know
And the world I fear
Threaten to meet.

3.

There is always a road,
The sea, dark hair, *dolor*.

Always a question
Bigger than itself—

      They say you're leaving Monday.
      Why can't you leave on Tuesday?

Christina Springer

Exile Propriety

Pretty Johnny Sinclair tore up
the country club golf course;
screwed vodka-valium junkie
Jilly-bean Jonquil until she bled;
and drunk drove home.

The police called.
His embarrassed parents smugly said:
boys will be boys,
checkbook in hand. Performed
harsh words in front of the officers.
Grounded him to their condominium in Aspen,
Colorado for two whole weeks
with no credit cards. My brother

grew man tall in exile.
I remember him hyperactive lean.
Fragile as grinning watermelon
salt shakers nudged off of antique
store shelves when Black folks shatter
drop history for the sake of propriety.

More James Dean than Sidney Poitier,
Brian carved his way
out of tidy blue nooses;
and pressed dress khakis;
and the imminent danger of Theo Huxtablization.
He inked "fuck" deeply into every school desk.

Carlton imitates Fresh Prince;
LL Cool J turns gangster;
Brian grows six feet tall, darkly
sentimental and perversely inclined to being
big, black and visible in our minty-fresh,
newly integrated neighborhood.
But, he stole

my codeine and drank my entire bottle
of gynecologist-prescribed red wine.
I negotiated a settlement of Quaaludes

and street mystery revealed
if I didn't tell Mother. I floated
behind my witch doctor brother down

to Murray Avenue where the public school
kids did fascinating things.
Loiter. Linger. Smoke cigarettes
and look good. Brian, in Shaft persona,
told me not to talk to the white trash
numskulls from Greenfield.

I flipped my hair, knowledgeable
savvy. I knew
they couldn't afford to live
in our neighborhood, even though they persisted
in defending it from us anyway. Sure enough,

some yinzer sidles up to me. Husky
whisper, *do me nigger-bitch*, grabs
a boob and my hoochie. In an instant,
everybody was kung fu fighting,
Numchucks snap, cracking, and Brian
chooses a peculiar moment to celebrate
ethnic pride. He runs home.
Gets the elephant speargun.

Three police vans.
Brian was the only one taken.
At the station I slipped easily
into Standard American Snob. I knew
nothing about cheap urban statistics,
only that in our neighborhood,
boys will be boys.

The next day Brian vanished.
Bad seeds belong in the trash, even if
your own mother has to scoop them out.
She said he was a liability.
We do not talk about him often.
Never in public.

In Pittsburgh, Pennsylvania, *yinzer* is a slang word that has a meaning similar to *redneck*.

Christopher Stackhouse

Mete

That look, what undermines breath's pace—
diadem, sloping, reticular hair, pronounced intelligence
how embellished the drunken curve of the moth's

recursive slanting course, rendered by the cheek
surrendered, how elegant the length of neck
features, an adorned ear: a strand of hair behind it,

might this author address the mouth—
its soft signature cursive brand leaves an imprint
drawn by time's inclination toward the perfect

shape, but beyond creation, after the rhythmic pulse
an instructional touch, tell me author. How much
measure by measure, appropriation of scale, its value

corresponds, distance, depth of field detail—
implore the hands, every word used to describe the motion
her form implies against the air, mute, singular, prophetic—

this-ness, to hold such an abdomen, to stagger
before the foot of your treasure trail, the parting gift
where the head lay there in the cut a forgotten fossil.

Innocence, set your lenses on the tableau
smile sweet water from the quarry.
You are always so contemporary. And I am alone

watching you sculpt the seconds. Backstage
a bleeding center collapses, opens again to accommodate
a kiss . . . lover herein is possibility, the process by which

Nicole Terez

border town

every night
we bank our fires and wait.

eventually sleep scratches at the back door,
stubbled with radio static, barbed constellations,

the pale tuning of his face
smuggled across checkpoints

the bones chime
within stale envelopes of smoke—

it is only paraffin and crude flintwork,
but it is enough to creak our slow hinges open.

we hold him
for as long as we can

and so
we do not hear the doors click shut,

the glass shards beneath his soles
when he leaves,

or feel warmth in light that bleaches through
frail as crackling papyrus.

Amber Flora Thomas

Dress

I turn the dress loose—its hand-sewn collar,
its seven bodice buttons, the hem's frayed edge.

I follow each stitch as it slips
from its hold. I'll reconcile with time later

this habit of proceeding toward the smallest task
unhurried. My arms draw back, fanning

the massive skirt. I lay the sleeve pieces
to one side, unfold the waist ties and stretch them

flat, cut out the fringes of buttonholes,
lose hook & eye in my lap.

I'm pulling open this mystery,
knotted flaws where a seamstress hurried

over her error, threaded paths ending
in the hidden cusp of the waist, lint sewn

into a pocket's seam. I take it from intricacy,
from fragility, from a tenement of irreproachable

lightness. No dress for a shoulder to ease against,
a thigh burn on, none to take account

of the crescent curve an arm makes.
No angles coming to life on a hanger.

Just this current of bygones exhausting its hold.
A neck hole that gapes for form, for the body it fitted,

for sweats and perfumes, the hairs
caught willy-nilly in a fold, for the order

begetting size and season. No memory unhooks
down the breastbone's swell,

excusing me from today.

Samantha Thornhill

West Indian Girl Contemplates the Push

I fed up wit she jokin me wet paper bag of a city.
Dis dotish Yankee gyul.
See she body drape ova de ledge so?
Watch me fix she.

She pay me to show she de bowels of my nation.
My Shanty town.
But how she go joke my city carve from tin?
Watch mc fix she.

She tink ev'ryting small cuz it far far away.
Stupid Yankee gyul.
When I ax if we go walk down 3rd street she say *no way!*
So watch me fix she!

She point an say, *look de ragamuffins ova so.*
I say, *no, shiny tamarind seeds!*
She doh know who standin behind she yuh know!
Well watch me fix she.

She eyes sharp sharp so like dunce cap.
Stupid Yankee gyul.
White Yankee breasts flat like she gaze.
Watch me fix she.

It against white man law to push she yuh know?
Dis stupid Yankee gyul.
But my laws ole an come from de hills.
So watch me fix she.

She doh know who standin behind she yuh know?
Shiny tamarind seed.
Black gyul wit breasts like fists.
Yes, I go fix she.

Venus Thrash

Wild Like That

Not our spit, not our seed, not our blood
Could arise from the darkness of this crime
No black boys since Scottsboro withstood
Justice didn't save those boys in time
Justice won't be swift to rescue us
From the clutch of history's dark lot
From the stigma of our father's lust
To be young, wild, and black in Central Park
Youth stolen in one bloody night
Guilty is the judgment by default
This strange fruit was not yet ripe
Black bodies hanging on this assault
We bear the burden of Cain's attack?
Not wild like that, not wild like that, not wild like that

Natasha Trethewey

Miscegenation

In 1965 my parents broke two laws of Mississippi;
they went to Ohio to marry, returned to Mississippi.

They crossed the river into Cincinnati, a city whose name
begins with a sound like *sin*, the sound of wrong—*mis* in Mississippi.

A year later they moved to Canada, followed a route the same
as slaves, the train slicing the white glaze of winter, leaving Mississippi.

Faulkner's Joe Christmas was born in winter, like Jesus, given his name
for the day he was left at the orphanage, his race unknown in Mississippi.

My father was reading *War and Peace* when he gave me my name.
I was born near Easter, 1966, in Mississippi.

When I turned 33 my father said, *It's your Jesus year—you're the same
age he was when he died.* It was spring, the hills green in Mississippi.

I know more than Joe Christmas did. Natasha is a Russian name—
though I'm not; it means *Christmas child*, even in Mississippi.

Lyrae Van Clief-Stefanon

Maul

Boy, you love like a tornado,
      got me spinning round and round.
Boy, your love's like a tornado,
      got me spinning round and round.
It's a shame, I don't know, sugar,
      when or where you'll put me down.

You can fry my catfish, daddy,
      just make sure your oil is hot.
Come and fry my catfish, baby,
      but make sure the grease is hot.
Boy, I got your side meal ready.
      Grits are bubblin' in the pot.

Go'n and take that train to Quitman.
      Honey, leave me if you must.
Catch Amtrak to Union Station.
      Baby, leave me if you must.
But just come back for me, sugar,
      or I'll crumble into dust.

I'ma smoke this pack of Pall Malls,
      then I'm gonna let you go.
Let me smoke this one last Pall Mall,
      I'll be good to watch you go.
I might set myself on fire
      just to show you so you'll know.

'Bout to go dig up some bloodroot,
      then I'm gonna shake your hand.
Need to slick my palm with bloodroot
      then I'll offer you my hand.
When you wake from your sweet slumber
      you'll be bound to be my man.

Boy, your heart is like a glacier,
        but to hell with all advice,
I'm gonna stick with you 'til I fall through
        a crevice in this ice.

Come & split my firewood, baby,
        with your heavy maul.
Come on split my firewood, baby.
        Honey, bring your heavy maul.
Way you turn 'way from me, daddy,
        It's go'n be a hard, cold fall.

Wendy S. Walters

Prophet as Slow Bird

Paper reads "Brown Pelicans Shot" along the coast
of Malibu. No one knows if it is a ritual sacrifice,
but birds are not harmless if one loves them and,
as well, deserve their fate. Dunlins and Godwits boast
of having seen the killer and whisper mis-advice
about the assassinations: birds were shot for being brown.
I smile at the other black girls in the liquor store, a band
of lovelies, but they do not know I want most
to be part of the brood, even though my look is imprecise.
Police come around asking questions, check my hands
for gunpowder, threaten witnesses, misread my frown
as proof. I watch those girls fly, like a skein of geese,
while cops make me promise to not leave town—
I worry about my alibi, the vulnerability of peace.

Nagueyalti Warren

Silver Rights

The girls and the boys stood side by side
white spittle staining their round brown
freshly open faces and starched smiles.

Looking over picket mothers in a line
soprano voiced these soldiers sang
We, O, we shall not be moved just like

Just like Lana blood oozing from a head wound
would not be moved when called *nigger*
would not from the lunch counter move

to eat at the Colored hole in the wall out back
Just like a tree planted by the rivers of water
that stubborn bleeding skinny girl would not.

Just like Willie Peacock would not stop
going into town, praying on courthouse grounds
police dogs at his back ready to attack the boy
on bended knees insisting he was free.

Glory hallelujah.

The boys and the girls who would not stop
went marching straight as trees
into the valley and shadows of death.

Afaa Michael Weaver

Charleston

In a fountain at the harbor, children
wash themselves in water spraying
in the heat. They count themselves dark
and light. The aircraft carrier sits
in the moist nothing of saltwater, tons
of tons weighing in the soft splash.
We count our wishes, to be free,
to be at ease, to be in abundance.
Above us spirits whirl in a thunderhead.

On steps across from the slave mart,
I peel an orange for the slow rip of its flesh
in my thumb, the sweet dotting of my nose
with its juice. I suck the threads of it,
gaze at the wooden doors now closed,
at the empty space inside with iron hooks.
I can see the white folks' heads checking
available cash in front of naked Africans
chained, bereaved, and listening to
a cruelty yet to be born. I can smell
the congregation of odors, humans fresh
from slave ships or working in fields, and
humans fresh from beds of fine linen,
sleeping with fingers in Bibles and prayers.

This is not a petty thing because we have
a rental car with an air conditioner, a tape
player, and various cushions. We have come
far to do this, to gaze out from the banks
of this plantation river to the rice fields,
to walk in Charleston. I keep the heat
from threatening my life, and I wonder
if I could have survived slavery to be old,
if being old is all there is to live to be.

I walk around the slave quarters and hear
African languages speaking in magnolias.

I hear the day's work being discussed
along with parents scolding children for
being children, as horror sifts above.
I hear wailing for children who are lost.

The avenues of ancient oaks are pillars
through to the past, the past of what is present.
We drive through the overhanging moss,
as wealth lingers beyond Sherman's burning.
It lingers in the eyes of black gardeners
who snip and shear carefully, lifting their eyes
to search for who cares that Africa is here.
I take these things as signs that miracles
always manifest in our ancestry when we
feel the need to touch the lights in the fire.

259 Brooklyn Avenue

I.

259 Brooklyn Avenue, WARWICK, named after a 14th-century
Military leader, is guarded by a band of black boys, conscripts
Of their own gang, where they're forced to wear their blood
Reversed. They stand out front spilling smoke from their mouths,
Shrinking or swelling in size depending on the hour or weather.
Inside, they sit by a perfect mouth of gold-capped mailboxes,
On the first landing of stairs that coil through the neck
Of the five-floor building, and make a seat of the radiator,
With the curves of a French horn, humming out a discordant
Steam; roll their blunts on the window's lips and dump
The cigars' insides in a mound of Backwoods mulch.

II.

259 became a torch the day 5C burned. It was a protest against those
That did not pay attention to the soft spots in the ceiling, dribbling rain
And melted snow onto hardwood floors. To the wires that unfurled,
Exposed frayed and disconnected nerves, to the children knifing their names
Into its walls. It was a protest to leak gas and light a cigarette. Consume
Roaches, rats and residents with its flamed canines. Belch a combustible blaze
That turned the eyes of other buildings phosphorescent. Perfume the hallways
With acrid pheromones, ink the air with ash and deposit cinders on everyone's
Pillow, that some packed up and left.

III.

When the cauterized hole cooled, 5C was a beauty mark on 259's cheek;
Its interior, terra cotta artifacts glazed and painted storm, eventually
Turned truants' quarters by that band of black boys. And when I pass
Through their hooded eyes, roughly stoned carved bodies and laughter
Morphed into coded tongue, we watch each other knowing the rooms
We share, exchanging hello with cotton-mouthed good evenings.

IV.

Only tree near 259 is outside my bedroom, charred branches unable to fully
Reproduce; knotty arthritic fingers almost knocking at window, shadows grab
Naked walls, my lover's body and me and rock with us. Even with the curtains
Closed on its voyeuristic leaves, on full moons and when helicopter searchlights
Illuminate rooftops, it edges forward and peers through the diaphanous cloth.

V.

Some woman's man has a cantankerous love affair with 259. Kicking
And chipping its skin, swelling its halls with bellicose rants, and punching
Holes in its windows. When the sun shines through cracked glass, rainbow
Bruises mark the walls. He sits on the steps, sipping Newport, holding
The banister like a thigh, a breast, the small of the back, like another hand
That meets in prayer and quiets his angry fist.

VI.

259 is seized in an epileptic fit when 4C washes clothes; its antennae stick out
Of nappy tar like picks, Timberlands drum across ceiling sending gunshot
Signals into blacken sky, while laying cumbersome feet on dreams. Radiators
Pipe out harmattan heat, each hour bodies shed covering. Sirens release
Silence, and 259 grows out of concrete, herniated vertebrae in a scoliotic spine.

Simone White

The Early Brilliance of Dwayne

One night in 1993
he called her on the telephone
through a tenement window
jerked off lavishly then walked over in the rain.
He let her read the Faulkner she was slaving over
interrupting with questions sometimes.
He knew Faulkner but mostly sat quiet for hours
til he took her by the neck
and into her teeth said *open your mouth*.

No credit for *haunches* but *skittish* and *colt*
impressively signal knowing too early
when a slick new heart falls open
for an instant you can hold it in your hand
the two halves needing to be joined
back to themselves but only by you
the hum of her throttle but not her berserk
the pleasures in the sounds it makes
just before it buckles.

Carolyn Beard Whitlow

Book of Ruth

> *Whither thou goest . . .*

      I learn to live by guile, to do without love.
I'm not scared. I wait in the dark for you,
Sleeping to avoid death, tired of sleep.
      The withered dyed rug fades, dims, fades, recolors,
      Warp frayed, weft unraveled; as light looms dark,
I doubt I'm happy as can be in this house.

      Outside no one would guess inside this house
I learn to live by guise, disguise my pain. Love
Dinner served by pyre light, sit doused by dark,
      Cornered in my room, wait in the dark for you.
      The bureau melts to shadow; that unraveled, uncolors.
Sleep to avoid death, tired of sleep,

      I avoid the mirror, the lie of truth. You sleep
Downstairs, chin lobbed over, chair rocked, spilled, house
Distilled in techtonic dreams of technicolor,
      Mostly golf course green and Triumph blue. I love
      Earthpots, cattails, a fireplace, no reflection of you.
While you sleep, I sip steeped ceremonial teas, dark

      As coffee, your swirled wineglass breathing dark
Downstairs fumes in the living dead room. Sleep
Comes easy, comes easy. I'm not scared. For you
      I curtsy before your mother, say I love this house.
      I love this house, this room. I love this. I love.
The traffic light blinks black and white. No color.

      Come Monday, I'll dustmop, repaper with multicolor
Prints, zigzag zebra stripe rooms, fuchsias, no dark
Blue or sober gray, none of the colors that you love.
      Insomnia is sweet, I think, the once I cannot sleep:
      I'm not scared. I'm not scared. This is my house.
Illumined by darkness, I watch my dark mirror you.

No. No silent hostage to the dark, I know you
Cast a giant shadow in a grim fairy tale, colors
Bloodlet, blueblack, spineless yellow trim this house;
       Escaped maroon, I emerge from a chrysalined dark,
       Succumb, mesmered under a light spring-fed sleep,
Nightmare over, giddy, without sleep, with love.

       The colors of the room fade into dust, house now dark.
I'm not scared. I learn to live without you, with love,
       To do without sleeping to avoid death.

Karen Williams

These Bones

In memory of the lives unearthed at the African Burial Ground, New York City, 1991
                                                    —*Lower Manhattan, 1712*

Under low-hanging trees
near lips of Collect Pond,
the ritual took place:
the carrying and wrapping
of the body, the placing
of shining bronze coins on the eyes,
the internment in sacred space.
The dark, muscled body,
like earth, a pillar,
glean of the Sankofa bird.
The mourners believed
the sage creature flew overhead,
winged toward Africa,
a full-bellied moon
while looking backward, a
perfect, tiny egg in its mouth.
The egg, content and shell,
trembles, cries:

> *Se wo were fi na wosan kofa a yenki*
> *Se wo were fi na wosan kofa a yenki*
> *It is not taboo to go back*
> *and fetch what you forgot.*
> *It is not taboo to go back*
> *and fetch what you forgot.*

And perhaps this limpid morning
mourners went back and fetched,
prayed and threaded
work-blistered hands
into each other's
and danced a hallowed ring shout,
their weariness hunched

low to the ground,
their hard flat feet
pounding earth,
sting of coffle,
cat-o-nine tail
into dust. They move
counterclockwise in tight circles,
bend their knees, moan
and billow their spines,
make guttural sounds.

A unique bay mourning makes,
the selection, unwrapping
and telling of memory as
blue-threaded palms, a thick stick
beat against
the soft, dry earth,
stories of pitted bones in it
becoming drumskin,
a chant, lifeblood that washes
Collect Pond gleaming,
until this worn, compressed father
of tilted shoulder, torn ligament,
kind and loving past once future,
is swaddled in white linen,
placed into pine
and lowered
into ground.

Another cry pierces
tender night, candlelight
fills the jeweled ears of
both mourner and dead,
copper shroud pins among them,
cowrie, shallow white shell,
delicate horn
button to decorate a father's grave,
an offering like water and fruit,
the caw of the Sankofa bird.

Dusk-flecked,
the bird warns mourners,

the fertile egg in its mouth,
us, the rememberers
to cry loud and spare not,
never forget story.
Sanctified,
these bones and earth.

Treasure Williams

prescription *or* for what ails you *or* poetry on demand

> *right now something*
> *to lift my spirits would be great. something that*
> *reminds me that i can make it better for me. hope i'm*
> *not sounding gloomy, some days are just so busy that*
> *i lose myself in it. let's talk more.*
> > *—crystal Redmond*

sister
i need some poetry to hope my heart
i need my poetry to be
non addictive
i need poems

i need a quip quickly
a quote quarterly

i need something
that will fit on a bumper sticker
or a pin

something i can read instead of a daily devotional
something that will get them niggas at work off my back

i need a poem better than my vibrator
even better than somebody else's man

i need a poem that will
go with a bad ass purse and stilettos

a poem girl

a poem i can light during a long hot bath

a poem that smells like musk
lavender
a hint of patchouli

a poem that smells better than the jacket he left in my closet

i need a poem that will keep me from
getting pregnant a poem

that is hormone free
and pro-choice

i need a poem for blackgirlswho'veconsideredtuballigationwhenthepillwasn'tenough

i need a poem that reduces the size of fibroids

and for gods sake a poem that doesn't promote yeast

i need a jet black poem
a dangerous we shouldn't be doing this poem

a that was the best head ever poem
a ladies' night drinks are free poem

a jimmy choo shoe 99% off poem

a baby let me get that poem
a you don't look a day over thirty poem

an i can still wear a belly shirt poem

a ben and jerry's whole pint poem

a really bad romance novel thoroughly read poem

a mental health sick day off to shop poem

a this outfit is so expensive i hid the receipt poem

a high school boyfriend seeing me and saying i should have married you poem

a best gay boyfriend poem

an end of the day and i take my bra off poem

a peace poem

a healthy poem

but most of all a poem that will never make me cry

Bridgette A. Wimberly

Garden of Eden Blues

A woman wears her heart baby, say she wears it like a carnation, red
A woman wears her heart baby, sits on her breast like a carnation, red
Leave my side sweet daddy, gonna wear a white carnation instead.

Say a woman's like a flower baby, petals soft and dewy sweet
This woman's like a flower, my petals soft and dewy sweet
Come water my garden won't you daddy, don't let me wither in this heat.

In life's garden baby, a lot of flowers grow.
Don't pluck me in the springtime, in the winter re-plow these rows.
Don't call me rose baby, treat me like daffodil.
Need some prunin' and some trimmin', I could give you such a thrill.

Say a woman wears her heart baby, sits on her breast like a carnation, red
Leave my side sweet daddy, gonna wear a white carnation instead.

Yolanda Wisher

Nola

the main character in Spike Lee's film She's Gotta Have It

How many nights I have lain in bed
thinking of you, Nola Darling.
I climb the fire escape from two floors below to see you
soaking your stained panties in the sink,
frying your liver and onions.

I have seen you naked in the bathroom,
raising my eyebrows at the secret of your stretch marks.
Watched you scrape the calluses away,
pluck the forked eyebrows,
shave the legs, thighs, and chin.
On Sundays, I expect the smell of texturizer,
wet heat in your hair.

I trail you to the supermarket,
know your weekday list well: lemons for your iced tea,
mango (fresh or sugared, for a treat),
bread, fish to fry, and salad dressing—if it's on sale.
Once, two years ago, you were short a dime
for a pack of gum and yogurt on your way to work;
I rescued you, the silver sweating with my hunger.

Nola, Nola, Nola.
Devil's floozied mistress. Hot, panting stray.
I could never take you home to my mother.
I would have to send you to wardrobe,
call in makeup, shine the soft lights liberally
to sop up the oil of your seduction.

Inside your little space,
I've watched a humble church rock
with a congregation of one, sometimes two,
your bed a sinner woman's pulpit,
your body an aisle for conniptions.

O bronze heifer, do you think of me and my yearnings?
Everything you do seems for someone else.
Soon, I will be bold enough
to climb through the window,
wearing nothing but my boots
to trod your hidden wet funk.

You'll fight me, won't you?
Your monstrous hands will throw me down,
you'll laugh, and I'll see the silver fillings
in the back of your mouth,
taunting riches to run my tongue over.

And I've brought the wine,
white, and strong enough
to cut through black memory.
Dissolve the rough edges, make you safe for me.
Tonight, I own this free stink spiraling into the city.
I ride your bed of candles,
lapping the cork off your skin,
the bright red from your lips.
Pull the scarf from your head.
Relish you.

Bitch, I have seen you choose randomly.
Who I am doesn't matter.

Toni Wynn

Good News from the River

What about that boy,
seven years old,
rescued in the river?

Did you hear his first words
when evening light
hit his calm little face?

I'm thirsty.
And he waved.
Everybody else—

his daddy, his uncle,
his brother—was all right
for hours, bundled dry.

But the boy's uncle
refused to leave the water
'til something was certain

about his nephew in the cabin
of that flipped boat.
The uncle sat

in a dinghy nearby,
just quiet, the whole four hours
the rescue crew worked.

Don't you feel like they
were spirit in the water
then, those two? And

that you want to do that
for somebody,
save or carry them

in deep love?
Stay on the river,
hold the shining space?

Al Young

To Go for Broke

To go for broke, in the gospel sense, means going
for the gold, going for good, going for God.
Onlookers sometimes wonder how blues people
or rhythm & blues people or even bad news people
can suddenly do the old-fashioned twist on a dime
and start preaching. Or, like Little Richard, how can they,
how dare they close a show and shout, "I have been saved"?
Unlike a document enslaved to commands, converts
don't need a flash of lightning or a whole lot of shaking
or incense going on. To go for broke, in the gospel sense,
means giving up everything you've got (or thought
you had) to God. Give up everything you were (or thought
you were) to the Lord. Give up everything you did
(or used to do) to Jesus. Once the Spirit eases in, look out!
God breaks the house—your duplex, your studio, your bungalow,
your flat, your town house, your beach house, your country estate
—and moves you into one of those lo! many mansions.
Al Green sings, "Take me to the river. Wash me down."
A person once given to Saturday night religion one day
becomes the same one who'll shake your glad hand Sunday.
And the same Creator who produces the show, lets you
script, direct and star in it, too. Spare no expense. Go for broke.

Kevin Young

Hard Headed Blues

Me & the Devil are rivals
for God's affection.

I can't say who wins.
My father's name

is Fate,
my son's Sin.

My guard dog's got laryngitis
& knows just one trick—

how to let folks in.

Came home early to find
my fiancée stolen—

her ring's gone to pawn
& my television's walked off—

Can't say I mind
that girl's gone

& that crackerjack ring wouldn't
cut anything

but why take my Zenith
with the good reception

& leave the one
with sound alone?

I tried but God's
still unlisted.

I don't mind using
love letters for fire

but at least leave me
some whiskey

to fan it higher.

Order your air-
conditioned coffin today.

I'm sick of listening
to beauty

pageants, I can't say
who wins. They keep on

rescheduling Armageddon

but only seats I can get
are in the nosebleed section.

Even Heaven
has evictions.

By accident
my obit ran early

& only the taxman
& that damn dog showed

to mourn me,
his bark's mute trumpet

my only eulogy.

Contributors

M. Eliza Hamilton Abegunde is a priestess, healer, and poet. Her fellowships include Sacatar (Brazil), Ragdale, and Norcroft. Her work has been published in *Margin Magazine, nocturnes (re)view of the literary arts, Wicked Alice, Warpland: A Journal of Black Literature and Ideas,* and *Beyond the Frontier: African-American Poetry for the Twenty-first Century.* She is the author of four chapbooks, including *Wishful Thinking* and *Contemporary Urban Prayer.* She is also the author of *The Ariran's Last Life* and *Tell Them Arroyo Sent You: Retracing the Routes of My Ancestors.*

Opal Palmer Adisa considers herself a griot who not only records the African Diasporic history but also writes the truths that have been buried. A poet and novelist, storyteller and mother, lover and adventurer, Adisa believes poetry is a balm, a toast, a praise song, and an invitation to love. Her latest poetry collection, *Caribbean Passion,* was published in 2004; her novel, *It Begins with Tears,* was published in 1997.

Elizabeth Alexander is the author of four books of poems (*American Sublime* most recently), a play (*Diva Studies*), and a book of essays (*The Black Interior*), among other works. She has been part of Cave Canem from the beginning. She teaches at Yale University. She is a member of the Cave Canem faculty.

Lauren K. Alleyne hails from the twin-island Republic of Trinidad and Tobago. Her work has appeared in the *Caribbean Writer,* the *Hampden Sydney Review,* and *Sexing the Political: A Journal of Third Wave Feminists on Sexuality* and is forthcoming in the *Atlanta Review.* She is the 2003 winner of the *Atlantic Monthly*'s Student Writing Contest and an International Publication Award from the *Atlanta Review.* She is coeditor of *From the Heart of Brooklyn,* a collection of student fiction, poetry and drama.

Holly Bass is a writer and performance artist based in Washington, D.C.

Venise N. Battle originates from Minnesota. She graduated from the University of Pennsylvania with a Bachelor of Arts in English and urban poetry. Battle attended Tufts University, where she completed her Master of Arts in teaching in 2005. She became a Cave Canem fellow in 2004.

Herman Beavers has taught courses in African American literature and creative writing at the University of Pennsylvania since 1990. He is completing work on a collection of poems entitled *Giving up the Ghost,* as well as a collection of prose poems. Born and raised in the Cleveland, Ohio, area, he now lives in Burlington, New Jersey, with his wife, Lisa, and their children, Michael and Corinne.

Michelle Courtney Berry (at Cave Canem from 1997 to 1999) is a poet, playwright, teacher, performer, actor, and the poet laureate of Tompkins County. Her work has appeared in *nocturnes, Random House,* the *Paterson Literary Review, Cokefish, Obsidian II, Pocketful of Poetry, Wells College Press,* and the Gannett newspapers. She has opened for Maya Angelou, Gayle Danley, and Howard Zinn. She lives a block away from the amazing Lyrae Van Clief-Stefanon in Ithaca, New York.

Tara Betts hopes to craft words that matter most to people she cares about. Her work has appeared in numerous publications and also in Steppenwolf Theatre's *Words On Fire,* HBO's *Def Poetry Jam,* and jessica Care moore's *SPOKEN.* She works with youth in Chicago and is pursuing her MFA at New England College. Her latest activities may be found at www.tarabetts.net.

Angela A. Bickham earned her MFA from the University of Notre Dame, her MA (in American studies) from the College of William and Mary, and her BA (in English) from the University of Virginia. Under her maiden name of Williams, Bickham has been published in *Role Call, Brothers and Others,* the *Xavier Review, Obsidian II, Obsidian III,* the *Black Scholar,* and the *Journal of African Travel-Writing.*

Remica L. Bingham, a native of Phoenix, Arizona, received her Master of Fine Arts degree from Bennington College. In addition to Cave Canem, she has attended the *Callaloo* creative writing workshops. Currently, she is working on a series of essays examining the intersections between hip-hop and contemporary poetry, as well as her first book, entitled *Conversion.* Her work has appeared in *PMS* and *New Letters.*

Shane Book was educated at the University of Western Ontario, the University of Victoria, New York University, the Iowa Writers' Workshop, and Stanford, where he was a Wallace Stegner Fellow in poetry. His work appears in many anthologies, including *Bluesprint, Role Call: A Generational Anthology of Social and Political Black Literature and Art, Why I Sing the Blues,* and *Breathing Fire 2: The New Canadian Poets.* He has been published in numerous journals, including *Fence, Volt,* and *Boston Review,* and his honors include an Academy of American Poets Prize, a *New York Times* Fellowship, the *Malahat Review* Long Poem Prize, the San Francisco State Poetry Center's Rella Lossy Poetry Award, the Charles Johnson Award, and a National Magazine Award.

Angela Brooks was born and raised in Memphis, Tennessee, where she lives with her husband, David, and three children, Sean, Genevieve, and Nile. She teaches ninth-grade English and, like so many other women, struggles to steal moments for writing. Her ongoing project is recording the oral histories of Memphis's black domestics. She owes so much to these women, who are taking the real story of the South to their graves.

Derrick Weston Brown is a Charlotte, North Carolina, native who currently resides in Mount Rainier, Maryland. Derrick recently received his

MFA in creative writing from American University. He has participated in several workshops and retreats, such as the Cave Canem workshop and the Squaw Valley Community of Writers workshop. He has performed as a featured poet at venues throughout the D.C.-Maryland-Virginia area and has served as a featured panelist on *The Workshop with Tony Medina*, a once-a-month radio show on Howard University's radio station, WHUR. He works full-time at a bookstore and as a writing counselor at American University.

Jericho Brown is a student in the University of Houston's Ph.D. program in creative writing and literature and a member of the New Orleans–based NOMMO Literary Society. His poems have appeared in *Callaloo* and *Role Call*.

Toni Brown's poems and stories have been published in journals and anthologies including *Night Bites: Vampire Stories by Women; Night Shade: Gothic Tales by Women; Pillow Talk II;* and most recently *Fireweed,* the *American Poetry Review, Philadelphia Poets,* and *Prairie Schooner.* She is an editor of *Painted Bride Quarterly* and the recipient of a Leeway Foundation Emerging Writers poetry grant.

Gloria Burgess celebrates the oral traditions of her African, Cherokee, and Scotch-Irish ancestors. Featured on NPR's *All Things Considered* and in a PBS film on social activism and the arts, Burgess's poetry also appears in diverse anthologies and journals. She is an affiliate professor at the University of Washington and principal consultant of Jazz, Inc., and her poetry books include *The Open Door* and *Journey of the Rose;* she has also written a book about her father's relationship with William Faulkner.

C.M.Burroughs lives in Pittsburgh, Pennsylvania, and is a K. Leroy Irvis Fellow in the MFA program at the University of Pittsburgh. Her poetry and writings have appeared in the *Wabash Review,* the *Curbside Review, Red Clay, Cave Canem Anthology IX,* and most recently the *Texas Poetry Journal.*

Lucille Clifton's books of poetry include *Blessing the Boats: New and Selected Poems 1988–2000,* which won the National Book Award; *The Terrible Stories* (1995), which was nominated for the National Book Award; *The Book of Light* (1993); *Quilting: Poems 1987–1990* (1991); *Good Woman: Poems and a Memoir 1969–1980* (1987), which was nominated for the Pulitzer Prize; *Two-Headed Woman* (1980), also a Pulitzer Prize nominee and winner of the University of Massachusetts Press Juniper Prize; *An Ordinary Woman* (1974); and *Good News about the Earth* (1972). She has also written *Generations: A Memoir* (1976) and more than sixteen books for children. Her honors include an Emmy Award from the American Academy of Television Arts and Sciences, a Lannan Literary Award, two fellowships from the National Endowment for the Arts, the Shelley Memorial Award, and the YM-YWHA Poetry Center Discovery Award. In 1999 she was elected a chancellor of the Academy of American Poets. She has served as poet laureate for the state of Maryland and is currently Distinguished Professor of Humanities at St. Mary's College of Maryland. She is a member of the Cave Canem faculty.

Taiyon Coleman's work has appeared in *Ethos; Knotgrass; Sketch; Drumvoices Revue; Sauti Mpya; Words Will Heal the Wound: A Celebration of Community Through Poetry, CD Volume II; Bum Rush the Page: A Def Poetry Jam; A View from the Loft; Maverick Magazine;* and the *Cave Canem Anthologies IV, V,* and *VI*. Currently, Coleman is a Ph.D. candidate in language and literature at the University of Minnesota.

Lauri Conner received her BA from the University of Kansas and her MFA from the University of Washington. She has taught English both at the secondary and the college level, working with a variety of writing applications, from creative to journalistic.

Curtis L. Crisler has an MFA in creative writing from Southern Illinois University, Carbondale. He has poetry forthcoming in the *Fourth River* and has been published in many magazines and journals, including *Sou'wester, Obsidian III, Warpland, Penumbra,* and *Callaloo*. He is a Cave Canem fellow and currently a limited-term lecturer at Indiana Purdue Fort Wayne.

Teri Ellen Cross was born in Cleveland, Ohio. She holds a Master of Fine Arts in poetry from American University; her work has appeared in *Bum Rush the Page, Beltway Quarterly,* and four Cave Canem anthologies. She currently produces a two-hour public talk-radio show in Washington, D.C. She resides in Silver Spring, Maryland.

Traci Dant holds an MFA in fiction from Washington University in Saint Louis. She is a 2003 MacDowell Colony poetry fellow and a 2002 Illinois Arts Council grant recipient. Her poetry has been presented at the Poetry Center of Chicago and published in the *Crab Orchard Review*. She was also a 2004 visiting writer at Trinity College in Connecticut.

Kyle G. Dargan is the former poetry editor for the *Indiana Review* and an advisory editor for *Callaloo*. His book, *The Listening,* won the 2003 Cave Canem Poetry Prize. He is originally from Newark, New Jersey.

Hayes Davis was born in Philadelphia, Pennsylvania, and holds a Master of Fine Arts in poetry from the University of Maryland. His work has appeared in Toi Derricotte's *The Black Notebooks, Bum Rush the Page,* and four Cave Canem anthologies; he was also a waiter at the Bread Loaf Writers' Conference. He currently teaches English and creative writing in Washington, D.C., and lives in Silver Spring, Maryland.

Jarita Davis earned a BA in classics from Brown University and both an MA and a Ph.D. in creative writing from the University of Louisiana, Lafayette. She was recently the writer in residence at the Nantucket Historical Association and has received fellowships from the Mellon Mayes program, Cave Canem, and Hedgebrook. In addition, she was awarded a Woodrow Wilson Travel Research Grant, as well as the Neiheisel Phi Beta Kappa Award. Her work has appeared in the *Southwestern Review, Historic Nantucket,* Cave Canem anthologies, and the *Crab Orchard Review*.

Kwame Dawes has published nine collections of poetry including *Progeny of Air* (winner of the Forward Poetry Prize) and *Midland* (winner of the Hollis Summers Poetry Prize). He is also a recipient of the Pushcart Prize and the Silver Musgrave Medal. Dawes's critical book on the lyrics of Bob Marley, *Bob Marley: Lyrical Genius*, remains one of the most authoritative books on Marley's art. Dawes is Distinguished Poet in Residence, Louise Fry Scudder Professor of the Liberal Arts, and executive director and founder of the South Carolina Poetry Initiative at the University of South Carolina. His children's book, *I Saw Your Face* (Dial), appeared in 2005. He is a member of the Cave Canem faculty.

Jarvis Q. DeBerry writes editorials for the *Times-Picayune* newspaper in New Orleans. He grew up on Old Highway 4 West near Holly Springs, Mississippi, a few miles away from "Junior's Place," the legendary joint where the late blues guitarist Junior Kimbrough encouraged wide-hipped women to "Do the Rump." Though DeBerry was far too respectable to visit Junior's, it never stopped him from fantasizing.

Toi Derricotte, a professor of English at the University of Pittsburgh, has published four books of poems, *The Empress of the Death House*, *Natural Birth*, *Captivity*, and *Tender*, winner of the 1998 Paterson Poetry Prize, and a memoir, *The Black Notebooks*. *The Black Notebooks* received numerous awards and was a *New York Times* Notable Book of the Year. She is the recipient of a Guggenheim Fellowship, two fellowships in poetry from the National Endowment for the Arts, and two Pushcart Prizes. She is the co-founder of Cave Canem.

Joel Dias-Porter (aka DJ Renegade) was born and raised in Pittsburgh, Pennsylvania. Widely published, in 1995 he received the Furious Flower Emerging Poet Award. He was the 1998 and 1999 Haiku Slam Champion. He has performed on the *Today Show*, on BET, and in the feature film *Slam*. The father of a young son, he has a CD of jazz and poetry entitled *LibationSong*.

Writer, vocalist, and Harlem denizen **La Tasha N. Nevada Diggs** has worked with many creative beings. Her literary and sound works have been used for projects ranging from Asian fetishes to Euro-House to hair books. The author of three chapbooks and one album, Diggs has received scholarships, residencies, and fellowships from Cave Canem, Harvestworks Digital Media Arts Center, the Naropa Institute, Caldera Arts, and the New York Foundation for the Arts. Diggs is currently the poetry curator for the online arts journal www.exittheapple.com. She enjoys writing, yodeling, tinkering with delay pedals, digital effects boxes, and cooking salmon cakes.

R. Erica Doyle's work has appeared in *The Best American Poetry*, *Ploughshares*, *Callaloo*, *Ms. Magazine*, *Bum Rush the Page*, *Gumbo*, *Contemporary Caribbean LGBT Writing*, and *Best Black Women's Erotica*. She has received awards from the Hurston/Wright Foundation and the Astraea Lesbian Writers Fund and collaborated with composer Joshua Fried to create *The Mirrored Fist*. She is at work on a novel, *Fortune*, and teaches English and creative writing in New York City.

Camille T. Dungy, author of *What to Eat, What to Drink, What to Leave for Poison* (Red Hen Press, 2006), has won fellowships and awards from organizations including the National Endowment for the Arts, the Virginia

Commission for the Arts, Cave Canem, the American Antiquarian Society, and the Bread Loaf Writers' Conference. Her work has appeared in the *Missouri Review*, the *Southern Review*, *Poetry Daily*, the *Mid-American Review*, the *Crab Orchard Review*, and other publications. She is the assistant editor of this anthology.

Cave Canem cofounder **Cornelius Eady** is the author of National Book Award finalist *Brutal Imagination* (2001); *Autobiography of a Jukebox* (1997); *You Don't Miss Your Water* (1995); *The Gathering of My Name* (1991); and *Victims of the Latest Dance Craze* (1985), the Lamont Poetry Selection of the Academy of American Poets. His honors include the *Prairie Schooner* Strousse Award and fellowships from the Guggenheim Foundation, the National Endowment for the Arts, the Rockefeller Foundation, and the Lila Wallace–Reader's Digest Foundation. His collaboration with jazz composer Diedre Murray has resulted in several theater works, including *You Don't Miss Your Water*; the Pulitzer Prize finalist *Running Man*; and two upcoming productions, *Fangs* and *Brutal Imagination.*

Michele Elliott is a writer, visual artist, and teacher. She is currently living in Washington, D.C., teaching writing for D.C. WritersCorps and the Corcoran College of Art and Design. She is a freelance grant writer, holds an MFA in creative writing from the University of Pittsburgh, and is a coeditor of the D.C. Poets Against the War anthology.

Born in Port-au-Prince, Haiti, **Phebus Etienne** grew up in East Orange, New Jersey. She completed writing programs at Rider University and New York University. Her poems have appeared in the *Crab Orchard Review*, *The Butterfly's Way: Voices from the Haitian Dyaspora in the United States*, the *Paterson Literary Review*, *The Best of Callaloo: Poetry*, and *Calabash*. She received a 2001 poetry fellowship from the New Jersey State Council on the Arts and a grant from the Whiting Foundation.

Chanda Feldman received an MFA in creative writing from Cornell University. Her poems have appeared widely in journals including the *Bellingham Review*, the *Florida Review*, and *Puerto del Sol*. Feldman is currently a production editor in San Francisco.

Nikky Finney is the author of three books of poetry, *On Wings Made of Gauze; Rice*, which won a PEN American Open Book Award; and *The World Is Round*. She is also the author of *Heartwood*, a collection of short stories, and is working on a novel. She has been published in several anthologies and was the scriptwriter for the documentary *For Posterity's Sake*, the story of Harlem photographers Morgan and Marvin Smith. She is an associate professor of creative writing at the University of Kentucky. She is a member of the Cave Canem faculty.

Reginald L. Flood is a Los Angeles native who now lives in New London, Connecticut. This poem is part of a manuscript entitled *Dancing on the Master's Table.*

Cherryl Floyd-Miller was the 2004 Fulton County Arts Council DIALOG Fellow in Atlanta. She has held writing residencies through Idyllwild,

Caldera, the Vermont Studio Center, and the Indiana Arts Commission. She is a produced playwright, her theater work mounted with the New World Stage theater and Western Michigan University. She is the author of two poetry collections—*Utterance: A Museology of Kin* and *Chops.* Floyd-Miller teaches creative writing at the Spruill Center for the Arts.

Krista Franklin is a poet, visual artist and educator who hails from Dayton, Ohio, and currently works and resides in Chicago. Her poems and art have appeared in/on several literary journals and Web sites, including the *Nexus Literary and Art Journal, Warpland, Obsidian III, nocturnes 2,* www.semantikon .com, www.milkmag.org, www.ambulant.org, and www.errataandcontradic tion.org. She has also been published in the anthologies *The Bust Guide to the New Girl Order* and *Bum Rush the Page* and is a Cave Canem alum.

John Frazier's work has been published in *Callaloo,* the *Gay and Lesbian Review Worldwide,* the *Beacon's Best,* the *New Republic,* the *Massachusetts Review,* the *Antioch Review,* and other journals. His book, *Bacco,* is a series of sonnets based on three Caravaggio paintings.

Deidre R. Gantt is a poet and fiction writer and a 2004 Cave Canem fellow. Her poems have previously appeared in *Brilliant Corners: A Journal of Jazz Literature* and *rolling out urban style weekly,* as well as on *Perspectives in Poetry,* an Atlanta-based public-access show. She now teaches community writing courses in her hometown, Washington, D.C., which is prominently featured in *Past Time,* her forthcoming chapbook.

Ross Gay has published poems in the *American Poetry Review,* the *Harvard Review,* the *Atlanta Review,* and *Margie: The American Journal of Poetry,* among others. He is a basketball coach, a demolition contractor, and a Philadelphia resident.

Regie O'Hare Gibson has read, taught, and lectured at universities and theaters in several countries. He and his work appear in *love jones,* a film based on events in his life. He is a National Poetry Slam champion, a *Chicago Tribune* Artist of the Year, and is regularly featured on NPR. His works have been published in journals and textbooks and translated into four languages. His book, *Storms Beneath the Skin,* is published by E. M. Press.

Carmen R. Gillespie is an associate professor of English at the University of Toledo. She is the author of the book *A Critical Companion to Toni Morrison* and is the recipient of the 2005 Ohio Arts Council Individual Artist Fellowship for Poetry. Her life has always been peopled with phantasms that reside only in the imagination and in the canyons and crevasses of narrative.

Aracelis Girmay writes poetry, fiction, and essays. Most recently, her poems and translations have appeared in *Rattapallax 11, 420pus,* and *Ploughshares.* She has been featured at the Bowery Poetry Club, Acentos, and the New Jersey State Prison, Trenton, among others. Girmay received her MFA from New York University, and currently resides in her native California, where she leads community writing workshops. Her picture book, *changing, changing,* is available through George Braziller.

Monica A. Hand is a poet and book artist currently living in New York City. She is the recipient of Maryland State and Montgomery County Individual Artist Awards. Her work can be found in Ethelbert Miller's *Beyond the Frontier* and in several online and print journals. In 2002 she printed a limited-edition handmade book of haiku, *Seven Seasons of Separation and Loss of Seven Seasons Lost*, in collaboration with artists Steven Stichter and Frederick Nunley.

Some of **Michael S. Harper**'s many titles include *Dear John, Dear Coltrane; Debridement; Images of Kin; Nightmare Begins Responsibility;* and *Songlines in Michaeltree: New and Collected Poems.* He edited *Chant of Saints* and, with Anthony Walton, *Every Shut Eye Ain't Asleep* and *The Vintage Book of African American Poetry.* Harper, the first state poet of Rhode Island, is a university professor, a New York Library Literary Lion, a Phi Beta Kappa scholar, and an American Academy of Arts and Sciences Fellow. He is the recipient of many distinctions, including the Robert Hayden Poetry Award from the United Negro College Fund, the Melville-Cane Award, and the Black Academy of Arts and Letters Award. He is a member of the Cave Canem faculty.

Heralded as one of three Chicago poets for the twenty-first century by WBEZ Chicago Public Radio, **Duriel E. Harris** is a cofounder of the Black Took Collective and the poetry editor of *Obsidian III: Literature in the African Diaspora. Drag* (Elixir Press), her first book, was hailed by *Black Issues Book Review* as one of the best poetry volumes of 2003.

Having lived in many U.S. metropolitan cities, **francine j. harris** is, at heart, a small-town poet. She has been published in many independent press magazines, such as *The Furnace* (Michigan), *Peregrine* (Massachusetts), and *blu* (New York). She has participated in various grassroots campaigns, performance-art collectives, and writing projects all over the country. She currently resides in Detroit, where she teaches poetry to eager high schoolers.

Reginald Harris's first book, *10 Tongues: Poems* (Three Conditions Press, 2002), was a finalist for the 2003 ForeWord Book of the Year and Lambda Literary Foundation Awards. His work has appeared in a variety of publications, including the journals *5 A.M., Black Issues Book Review, Gargoyle, Poetry Midwest,* and *Sou'wester* and the *Role Call* and *Bum Rush the Page* anthologies.

Yona Harvey's poems have appeared in *Callaloo, Ploughshares,* and *West Branch,* among other journals and anthologies. Born in southern Ohio, she currently lives in Pittsburgh, Pennsylvania, with her husband, Terrance Hayes, and their two children.

Terrance Hayes is the author of *Hip Logic* (Penguin, 2002) and *Muscular Music* (Tia Chucha Press, 1999) and has been a recipient of many honors, including a Whiting Writers' Award, the Kate Tufts Discovery Award, a National Poetry Series Award, a Pushcart Prize, a *Best American Poetry* selection, and a National Endowment for the Arts fellowship. *Wind in a Box,* his third collection, is forthcoming from Penguin in 2006. He met his wife, poet Yona Harvey, at the first Cave Canem retreat.

Tonya Cherie Hegamin is a proud Pennsylvanian, although she currently resides at Soul Mountain Retreat in Connecticut. Hegamin recently received an MFA in children's literature from the New School and works extensively with "at-risk" and institutionalized youth. She also holds a BA in poetry from the University of Pittsburgh. Two of her books, *Most Loved in All the World* and *M+O 4EVR*, are forthcoming from Houghton Mifflin.

Sean Hill was awarded a Michener Fellowship for poetry from the University of Houston's creative writing program. He has received scholarships to the Bread Loaf Writers' Conference, been awarded the Academy of American Poets Prize, and been nominated for a Pushcart Prize. His poems have appeared in *Callaloo, Painted Bride Quarterly*, the *Indiana Review*, the *lyric poetry review, Pleiades*, and the anthology *Blues Poems* (Everyman's Library). He lives in northern Minnesota.

Andre O. Hoilette is a Jamaican-born poet who lives and works in Ohio. He and his family immigrated to the United States in 1982. He has spent his formative years in America and has learned many hard lessons from this country.

Lita Hooper lives in Atlanta, Georgia. She is an associate professor of English at Georgia Perimeter College. Her work has appeared in *Role Call* and several journals. Her book, *The Art of Work: The Life and Art of Haki Madhubuti*, was published in 2005.

Erica Hunt is the author of three books of poetry, including *Arcade*, with artist Alison Saar, and *Piece Logic*. Her essay "Notes for an Oppositional Poetics," in Charles Bernstein's *The Politics of Poetic Form*, has put her in the forefront of experimental poets. She is a member of the Cave Canem faculty.

Kate Hymes is a poet and educator living in the Hudson Valley of New York State. She completed her third summer residency with Cave Canem in June 2004. Her work has been published in *Peregrine*, Cave Canem anthologies, and Hudson Valley regional publications. She is currently working on an anthology of memoir and poetry by black and white women writers who remember how race was lived in the United States before 1955.

Linda Susan Jackson is the author of two chapbooks, *Vitelline Blues* and *A History of Beauty*. Most recently her work has appeared in *Rivendell, Warpland, Brooklyn Review 21*, and *Brilliant Corners*, among other journals. Her awards include a fellowship to Cave Canem. She teaches at Medgar Evers College/City University of New York and lives in Brooklyn.

Major Jackson is the author of two collections of poetry, *Hoops: Longer Poems* and *Leaving Saturn*, a finalist for the National Book Critics Circle Award. His work has appeared in the *American Poetry Review, Callaloo*, the *New Yorker*, and *Triquarterly*. A recipient of a Whiting Writers' Award, he is an associate professor of English at the University of Vermont and teaches in the MFA creative writing program at Queens University of Charlotte in North Carolina.

Honorée Fanonne Jeffers is the author of two books of poetry, *The Gospel of Barbecue* (Kent State, 2000), which won the 1999 Stan and Tom Wick

Poetry Prize, and *Outlandish Blues* (Wesleyan, 2003). She has won an award from the Rona Jaffe Foundation and fellowships from the MacDowell Colony and the Bread Loaf Writers' Conference. Her poetry has been published in the *American Poetry Review, Brilliant Corners, Callaloo,* the *Iowa Review,* the *Kenyon Review, Ploughshares,* and *Prairie Schooner.* A native southerner, Jeffers now lives in Oklahoma, where she teaches at the University of Oklahoma.

Tyehimba Jess's first book of poetry, *leadbelly,* was a winner of the 2004 National Poetry Series. He received a 2004 Literature Fellowship from the National Endowment for the Arts and was a 2004–5 winter fellow at the Provincetown Fine Arts Work Center. He won a 2000–2001 Illinois Arts Council Fellowship in poetry and the 2001 *Chicago Sun-Times* Poetry Award. He was on the 2000 and 2001 Chicago Green Mill slam teams.

Amaud Jamaul Johnson was born and raised in Compton, California, and educated at Howard University and Cornell University. His honors include a Wallace Stegner Fellowship in poetry at Stanford University and a work-study scholarship from the Bread Loaf Writers' Conference. His poetry has appeared in *Rivendell* and the *New England Review* and on *Poetry Daily.* He teaches in the creative writing program at the University of Wisconsin–Madison.

Brandon D. Johnson, originally from Gary, Indiana, is a resident of Washington, D.C., a Larry Neal Writers' Competition awardee, a Cave Canem fellow from 1997 to 1999, and a 1999 D.C. Commission on the Arts and Humanities fellowship grant recipient. He has been published in *The Drumming Between Us, Winners, Drumvoices 2000,* and *Callaloo* and is the author of *Man Burns Ant* and *The Strangers Between* and coauthor of *The Black Rooster Social Inn: This Is the Place.*

Karma Mayet Johnson is a poet, performing artist, and percussionist. She resides in Brooklyn, New York, with her boa constrictor, Krishna. Recent work has been published in *African Voices Magazine, A Gathering of the Tribes,* and *nocturnes.*

A. Van Jordan's *Rise,* published in 2001 by Tia Chucha Press, won the PEN/Oakland Josephine Miles Award and was a selection of the Academy of American Poets book club. His latest book, *M-A-C-N-O-L-I-A,* was published in 2004 by W. W. Norton and Co. and won a 2004 Whiting Foundation award. He was also awarded the 2004 Robert Frost Fellowship at Middlebury College's Bread Loaf Writers' Conference. He currently serves as assistant professor of English at the University of North Carolina at Greensboro and on the faculty of the MFA Program for Writers at Warren Wilson College.

Carolyn C. Joyner's poetry has been featured in *Dialogue* and anthologized in *360 A Revolution of Black Poets, Edge of Twilight, Mass Ave Review,* and *Beyond the Frontier.* In May 2001, she received a Master of Arts degree in writing with a focus on poetry at the Johns Hopkins University. In 2003 and 2004, she was awarded fellowship grants by the D.C. Commission on the Arts and Humanities and the Virginia Center for the Creative Arts.

John Keene is the author of the novel *Annotations* and, with artist Christopher Stackhouse, of the chapbook *Seismosis*. His honors include fellowships from the Massachusetts Artists Council and the New Jersey State Council on the Arts. He teaches at Northwestern University.

Poet, fiction writer, scholar, and teacher **M. Nzadi Keita** is a first-generation urban northerner. Mother of two sons. Spouse. Cave Canem alumna. Her publications include the *American Poetry Review, Proteus, Beyond the Frontier: African-American Poetry for the Twenty-First Century, Bum Rush the Page*, and *Impossible to Change: Women, Culture, and the Sixties*. Recipient of poetry fellowships from the Pennsylvania Council on the Arts and fiction fellowships from Yaddo and the Ragdale Foundation, Keita teaches creative writing and literature at Ursinus College.

Ruth Ellen Kocher is the author of *One Girl Babylon* (New Issues Press, 2003); *When the Moon Knows You're Wandering* (New Issues Press, 2002), winner of the Green Rose Prize in poetry; and *Desdemona's Fire* (Lotus Press, 1999), winner of the Naomi Long Madgett Poetry Award. Her work has appeared in the *Washington Square Journal, Ploughshares*, the *Crab Orchard Review*, the *Clackamas Literary Review*, the *Missouri Review*, the *African American Review*, the *Gettysburg Review*, and *Antioch*, among other journals, including a Persian translation in the Iranian literary magazine *She'r*. She teaches literature and writing at the University of Missouri, St. Louis.

Yusef Komunyakaa won the Pulitzer Prize in 1994 for *Neon Vernacular: New and Selected Poems*, just one of his twelve books of poetry. His most recent works are *Talking Dirty to the Gods*, a finalist for the National Book Critics Circle Award, and *Blue Notes: Essays, Interviews and Commentaries*. Among his many distinguished poetry collections is *Thieves of Paradise*, a 1999 finalist for the National Book Critics Circle Award. He coedited (with Sascha Feinstein) *The Jazz Poetry Anthology* and *The Second Set: The Jazz Poetry Anthology, Volume 2*. He is also the author of *Slip Knot*, a libretto written in collaboration with the opera's composer, T. J. Anderson. Komunyakaa is a chancellor of the Academy of American Poets and a professor in the Council of Humanities and the creative writing program at Princeton University. He is a member of the Cave Canem faculty.

Jacqueline Jones LaMon is a poet and writer. Her work has appeared in publications including the *Crab Orchard Review*, the *Black Issues Book Review*, *African Voices*, the *Mosaic Literary Journal*, and *Warpland*. Currently a Chancellor's University Fellow at Indiana University, she is a graduate of Mount Holyoke College and the UCLA School of Law. LaMon is the author of the novel *In the Arms of One Who Loves Me* (One World/Ballantine).

Quraysh Ali Lansana is the director of the Gwendolyn Brooks Center for Black Literature and Creative Writing at Chicago State University, where he is also an assistant professor of English/creative writing; is the author of *They Shall Run: Harriet Tubman Poems* and *Southside Rain;* is the coeditor of *Role Call* (Third World Press, 2004, 2000, and 2002, respectively); and sits on the editorial board of Tia Chucha Press.

Carmelo Larose was born and raised in Brooklyn, New York. He is currently getting his Ph.D. in English at New York University while working on his first novel and book of poetry.

Virginia K. Lee lives in New York City. She is a Cave Canem graduate (2003). Her poems have been published in *African Voices, Wish Women*, and *Warpland*. Her work also appears in various anthologies, including *Brothers and Others*. Her chapbook is entitled *Sticks, Stones and Bones*. She is working on a manuscript entitled *What Price This Skin?*

Raina J. León, a member of the Carolina African American Writers' Collective, is currently a doctoral student in education at the University of North Carolina–Chapel Hill. Her work has been featured at the Cornelia Street Café, the Nuyorican Poets Café, the Bowery Poetry Club, Acentos at the Blue Ox Bar, and Bar 13 through the LouderArts Project. *AntiMuse* and the upcoming anthology by Gival Press, *Poetic Voices without Borders*, have also housed her work.

Doughtry "Doc" Long was born in Atlanta, Georgia, and grew up in Trenton, New Jersey. He has lived and worked in New York and Africa. His most recent publications include *Timbuktu Blues* (Palanquin Press, 2001), *Rules for Cool* (Xlibris, 2001), and the compact disk *We of Darker Light* (2003).

Kenyetta Lovings teaches adult literacy in the New York public libraries. Her written work can be seen in *Ambulant, Black Ivy, Sidereality: A Journal of Speculative and Experimental Poetry*, and *Warpland*. She currently resides in Harlem, New York, and studies literature at Sarah Lawrence College.

Adrian Matejka is a graduate of the MFA program at Southern Illinois University, Carbondale. His poems have appeared in the *Crab Orchard Review, Gulf Coast*, the *Indiana Review*, and *Painted Bride Quarterly*, among other journals and anthologies. His first collection of poems, *The Devil's Garden*, won the 2002 New England/New York Award from Alice James Books.

Shara McCallum is the author of two books of poems from the University of Pittsburgh Press, *Song of Thieves* (2003) and *The Water Between Us* (1999, winner of the 1998 Agnes Lynch Starrett Poetry Prize). Originally from Jamaica, McCallum directs the Stadler Center for Poetry and teaches at Bucknell University. She is also on the faculty of the Stonecoast low residency MFA program. She lives in Pennsylvania with her family.

Carrie Allen McCray was born in 1913 in Virginia. She received her AB from Talladega College and a master's from New York University. She has been a social worker and a college teacher. Her publications include the 1965 short story "Adjös Means Goodbye," which appeared in John A. Williams's *Beyond the Angry Black* and later in McDougal Littell's *Reading Literature* and was also produced at Luna Theatre in Montclair, New Jersey. She has published a memoir, *Freedom's Child* (Algonquin), and a chapbook of poetry, *Piece of Time* (Chicory Blue Press). Individual poems have appeared in *Ms. Magazine*, Cave Canem yearly anthologies, *Family Reunion*, and *Word of Mouth: Poems Read on NPR's* All Things Considered.

Ernesto Mercer is a welfare case manager in Washington, D.C. He is an alumni fellow of Cave Canem. He attended Cave Canem in 1996, 1997, and 1999. At present he lives in Mount Rainer, Maryland.

Dante Micheaux is an emerging poet whose work has appeared in *Warpland* and a previous Cave Canem anthology. He has been a guest poet of the Church of Saint John the Divine, the Publishing Triangle, and City X-Posed. In 2002, he received a prize in poetry from the Vera List Center for Art and Politics. He resides in New York City.

Jonathan Moody was born in Belleville, Illinois. He's lived in California and Germany. However, most of his childhood was spent in Fort Walton Beach, Florida. He received his BS degree in psychology from Xavier University of Louisiana. Moody is an MFA student at the University of Pittsburgh. His poetry has appeared in the *Xavier Review*.

Kamilah Aisha Moon is a Cave Canem fellow and a Paumanok Award semi-finalist. Her work has been featured in *Mosaic, Bittersweet,* the *Black Arts Quarterly, Open City, Phoenix, Bum Rush the Page, Warpland, OBSIDIAN III, Toward the Livable City,* and *Sable*. Featured in various conferences and festivals around the country, Moon is currently an MFA candidate at Sarah Lawrence College.

Indigo Moor is a native North Carolinian residing in Rancho Cordova, California. He is a 2002 recipient of Cave Canem's writing fellowship in poetry. Publication credits include the *Xavier Review*, Boston University's the *Comment*, and the Pushcart Prize–nominated *Out of the Blue Artists Unite*.

Lenard D. Moore, founder and executive director of the Carolina African American Writers' Collective, has been nominated twice for a Pushcart Prize. He is author of *Forever Home* (St. Andrews College Press, 1992). His poetry has appeared in several magazines and over forty anthologies. Recipient of the Margaret Walker Creative Writing Award (1997) and the Haiku Museum of Tokyo Award (2003, 1994, 1983), he has taught English, studies in modern poetry, and poetry writing at North Carolina State University. Currently, he teaches at Shaw University.

Harryette Mullen's poems, short stories, and essays have been published widely and reprinted in over forty anthologies. Her poetry is included in the latest edition of the *Norton Anthology of African American Literature* and has been translated into Spanish, French, Polish, and Bulgarian. She is the author of six poetry books, most recently *Blues Baby* (Bucknell, 2002) and *Sleeping with the Dictionary* (University of California, 2002). The latter was a finalist for the National Book Award, the National Book Critics Circle Award, and a *Los Angeles Times* Book Prize. In 2004, she received an award from the Foundation for Contemporary Performance Arts. She was born in Alabama, grew up in Texas, and now lives in Los Angeles, where she teaches at UCLA. She is a member of the Cave Canem faculty.

Marilyn Nelson's 2005 books are *Fortune's Bones*, published by Front Street Books, *A Wreath For Emmett Till*, published by the Houghton Mifflin children's division, and *The Cachoiera Tales and Other Poems*, published by Louisiana State University Press. Nelson is founder and president of Soul Mountain Retreat, a writers' colony; an emeritus professor of English at the University of Connecticut, Storrs; and poet laureate of the State of Connecticut. She is a member of the Cave Canem faculty.

Mendi Lewis Obadike's works include *Armor and Flesh* (poems); the Internet opera *The Sour Thunder;* and commissions from the Whitney Museum, Yale University, the New York African Film Festival, and Electronic Arts Intermix. She and her husband, Keith Obadike, received a Rockefeller Fellowship for the opera *TaRonda, Who Wore White Gloves*. She will launch *Four Electric Ghosts* at Toni Morrison's Atelier at Princeton. Mendi and Keith live and work in the New York metropolitan area.

Gregory Pardlo has received fellowships from the *New York Times*, the MacDowell Colony, and Cave Canem. His poems have appeared in *Callaloo, Lyric, Painted Bride Quarterly, Ploughshares*, the *Seneca Review, Volt*, and elsewhere. He has translated, from the Danish poet Niels Lyngso, *Pencil of Rays and Spiked Mace* (BookThug, 2004). He teaches at Medgar Evers College, City University of New York, in Brooklyn.

Carlo Toli Paul was born in Brooklyn, New York, to Haitian parents. His family moved to Maryland when he was six years old. His poems have appeared in Cave Canem's anthologies. He is a graduate of the University of Maryland, College Park, and his poems first appeared in the campus publications *Eclipse* and *Stylus*.

Gwen Triay Samuels is an ESL/bilingual teacher in the New Jersey public schools and a New Jersey–certified court interpreter and translator. She renewed her dedication to poetry in 1998 and has been published twice in the *Paterson Literary Review*. Gwen will be a second-year Cave Canem fellow in 2005 and hopes to publish her first collection of poetry soon.

Known as one of the leaders of the Black Arts Movement, **Sonia Sanchez** is a poet, activist, and scholar who has written sixteen books, including *Does Your House Have Lions?* (1997, nominated for the National Book Critics Circle Award for Poetry), *Like the Singing Coming Off the Drums: Love Poems* (1998), and *Shake Loose My Skin* (1999). Sanchez won the 2001 Robert Frost Award from the Poetry Society of America and the 1995 American Book Award for her book *Homegirls and Handgrenades*. She is also the recipient of an NEA Fellowship, the Community Service Award from the National Black Caucus of State Legislators, the 1998 Governor's Award for Excellence in the Humanities, and a Pew Fellowship in the Arts for 1992–93. She is a member of the Cave Canem faculty.

In addition to his latest book of poems, *Buffalo Head Solos*, **Tim Seibles** is the author of five other collections of poetry, including *Hammerlock* and *Hurdy-Gurdy*. He has received awards including an NEA Fellowship and an Open Voice Award from the Sixty-third Street Y in New York City. His work has been featured in anthologies such as *New American Poets of the '90s, Outsiders, The Poets Grimm, Verse and Universe*, and *A Way Out of No Way*. He lives in Norfolk, Virginia, where he teaches in Old Dominion University's English department and MFA in writing program. He is a member of the Cave Canem faculty.

Elaine Shelly is a Cave Canem fellow (1997–99) who lives in the Ohio outback. Her life has been saved many times by gentle poets and well-crafted poems.

Born in Los Angeles, **Cherene Sherrard** holds a BA from UCLA and a Ph.D. in English from Cornell University. She is an assistant professor of English at the University of Wisconsin–Madison. Her fiction, poetry, and literary criticism have appeared in *American Literature*, the *African American Review*, *5 A.M.*, *Obsidian II*, and *Dark Matter II: Reading the Bones*. In 2005, she received a Wisconsin Arts Board grant for her poetry manuscript *Girls Named Peaches*.

Kevin Simmonds is a native of New Orleans. His writings have appeared in the *American Scholar, Field*, the *Massachusetts Review, Poetry, Rhino*, and other publications. His stints as a teacher, conductor, composer, and singer have taken him throughout the United States, Japan, and the Caribbean.

Patricia Smith is the author of three poetry volumes—*Close to Death; Big Towns, Big Talk*; and *Life According to Motown*—as well as *Africans in America*, the companion book to the groundbreaking PBS series, and the award-winning children's book *Janna and the Kings*. She is currently at work on *Fixed on a Furious Star*, a biography of Harriet Tubman, to be published by Crown in 2006. She is a four-time National Poetry Slam champion, a featured poet on both *Def Poetry Jam* and www.defpoetry.com, and a Cave Canem faculty member.

Tracy K. Smith's book, *The Body's Question*, won the 2002 Cave Canem Poetry Prize and was published by Graywolf Press. She has also received awards from the Rona Jaffe and Ludwig Vogelstein Foundations, as well as a fellowship from the Bread Loaf Writers' Conference. She teaches at the University of Pittsburgh.

Christina Springer is a text artist giving voice to those unlarynxed by convention, conformity, or ignorance by using theater, dance, poetry, and multiple forms of visual expression. Recent work has been produced by the Composer Collaborative of New York and the Umoja African Arts Company. Recent poems have appeared in *Janus Head, Femspec*, and *The Complete Idiot's Guide to Slam Poetry*.

Christopher Stackhouse is a writer and visual artist. His poems and drawings have been published in the literary arts journals *Hambone, FENCE, Aufgabe, Bridge, Swerve, nocturnes*, and *Rattaplax*. *Seismosis* (2003), a collaboration of text by poet/writer John Keene and Stackhouse's line drawings was published as a handmade limited edition artist book by the Center for Book Arts (New York City). He is a poetry editor of *FENCE* magazine.

Nicole Terez was born and raised in Cleveland, Ohio. Her work has appeared in *Can We Have Our Ball Back?* and *Folio: A Literary Journal*. She currently lives in Boston, Massachusetts.

Amber Flora Thomas is the recipient of several major poetry awards, including the Richard Peterson Prize and the Ann Stanford Prize. Her poetry has appeared in *Calyx*, *Gulf Coast*, the *Bellingham Review*, and the *Southern Poetry Review*, among other publications. She has an MFA in poetry writing from Washington University in Saint Louis, where she won an Academy of American Poets Prize and a postgraduate teaching fellowship. Her first collection of poetry, *Eye of Water*, won the Cave Canem Poetry Prize and was published by the University of Pittsburgh Press in 2005.

Samantha Thornhill received her BA in creative writing from Florida State University and her MFA in poetry from the University of Virginia, where she received a Henry Hoyns Fellowship. A proud member of Cave Canem, Thornhill is also a nationally known performance poet. She is currently a teacher of poetry and performance in the Juilliard School's drama division. Her Web site is http://samanthaspeaks.com.

Venus Thrash received a BA in literature and an MFA in creative writing from the American University. She resides in Washington, D.C., and is currently at work on her short-story collection and her novel, *Hole*.

Natasha Trethewey is author of *Bellocq's Ophelia* (Graywolf, 2002) and *Domestic Work* (Graywolf, 2000). Her third collection is *Native Guard* (Houghton Mifflin). She is the recipient of fellowships from the Guggenheim Foundation, the Rockefeller Foundation Bellagio Study Center, the National Endowment for the Arts, and the Bunting Fellowship Program of the Radcliffe Institute for Advanced Study at Harvard. She is an associate professor of English and creative writing at Emory University and during the 2005–6 academic year held the Lehman Brady Joint Chair Professorship of Documentary and American Studies at Duke and UNC–Chapel Hill.

Lyrae Van Clief-Stefanon's first collection of poems, *Black Swan*, won the 2001 Cave Canem Poetry Prize. Her work has appeared in the *African American Review*, *Callaloo*, the *Crab Orchard Review*, *Shenandoah*, and other journals, as well as the anthologies *Common Wealth*, *Bum Rush the Page*, and *Role Call*. Currently at work on a second collection of poems, *Open Interval*, and a novel, *Six Ways from Sunday*, she is an assistant professor of English at Cornell University.

Wendy S. Walters was raised in suburban Detroit and has published poems in *Callaloo*, *Sou'wester*, the *Yalobusha Review*, the *Seneca Review*, *nocturnes*, and *nthposition.com*. *Birds of Los Angeles*, a chapbook of poems, was published by Palm Press. She has been a resident fellow at Yaddo and the MacDowell Colony and is assistant professor of English at the Rhode Island School of Design.

Nagueyalti Warren, a fellow from Atlanta, Georgia, is an educator and administrator at Emory University, where she has served as assistant and currently as associate dean of Emory College. She also teaches in the Department of African American Studies. Recently she completed an MFA in creative writing from Goddard College.

Afaa Michael Weaver (b. Michael S. Weaver) is the author of nine collections of poetry, most recently *Multitudes, The Ten Lights of God,* and *Sandy Point.* His plays have been produced professionally, and he has also published short fiction. In 1998 he was a Pew Fellow. From 1997 to 2000, he was editor of *Obsidian III.* He has studied and taught in Taiwan and China as a Fulbright scholar. Weaver has studied Taijiquan for twenty-six years and is a Dao disciple of Shifu Huang Chien Liang. He is a Cave Canem Elder and holder of an endowed chair at Simmons College, where he is the Alumnae Professor of English. He is a member of the Cave Canem faculty.

Arisa White is a native New Yorker, born and raised in Brooklyn. She received her MFA in poetry from the University of Massachusetts, Amherst. Her work has appeared in *Meridians, Crate Magazine, Failbetter.com, A Gathering of Tribes, African Voices,* and *Sarah Lawrence Magazine.*

Simone White is a Philadelphian and a lawyer. She attended Wesleyan University, Harvard Law School, and the New School's MFA program in creative writing. Shuttling between Philadelphia and New York, she writes poems and poemlike experiments that have appeared in the *Indiana Review* and in the online journal *Can We Have Our Ball Back?*

Carolyn Beard Whitlow's manuscript *Vanished* was a finalist for the 2005 Ohio State University Press Poetry Prize. Her poems have appeared in the *African American Review, 5 A.M.,* the *Kenyon Review,* the *Indiana Review,* the *Massachusetts Review, 13th Moon, Callaloo,* the *Dos Passos Review,* the *Crab Orchard Review,* the *Cold Mountain Review,* and others. She is the Charles A. Dana Professor of English at Guilford College in Greensboro, North Carolina.

Karen Williams is a bioethicist and writer specializing in issues of race, culture, health, and communications in Michigan. Widely published in many journals, newspapers, and anthologies, including *Beyond the Frontier* (Black Classics Press), she's currently researching and writing a television documentary on the history of African American health and a television Public Service Announcement series on multicultural health for an award-winning Boston production company.

A native of Meridian, Mississippi, **Treasure Williams** is a Memphis-based writer, freelance editor, journalist, MC, and emerging poet. She works full-time for the Memphis city schools as a high school English instructor and has received an MFA from the University of Memphis's creative writing program. The selected poem is from her poetry manuscript, *feeding the dead.*

Bridgette A. Wimberly is both a published and produced playwright and a poet whose work has been performed across the United States. Her first play, *Saint Lucy's Eyes,* was produced off-Broadway starring Ruby Dee. "Garden of Eden Blues" is featured in her play *The Separation of Blood,* about blood pioneer Dr. Charles Drew.

Yolanda Wisher lives in Philadelphia, where she teaches English at Germantown Friends School and sings jazz with the band When Malindy Sings. Her poetry has appeared in the *Sonia Sanchez Literary Review,* the

DrumVoices Revue, Meridians, nocturnes, Fence, Open Letter, and *Ploughshares.* In 1999, she was declared the first poet laureate of Montgomery County in Pennsylvania, where she grew up.

Toni Wynn writes poems and sometimes is astonished. Come visit: Hampton, Virginia, stucco house by the water. Bring the family.

Al Young is the author of more than twenty books, including *The Sound of Dreams Remembered: Poems 1990–2000,* the novel *Sitting Pretty,* and *African American Literature: A Brief Introduction and Anthology.* He has written scripts for Bill Cosby, Richard Pryor, and Sidney Poitier. Young is the recipient of Guggenheim, NEA, and Fulbright Fellowships and the American Book Award. He has been a visiting professor at many universities, including Rice, Michigan, Washington State, San Jose State University, and UC Berkeley. He is a member of the Cave Canem faculty.

Kevin Young's first book, *Most Way Home,* was selected for the 1993 National Poetry Series (by Lucille Clifton) and won the John C. Zacharis First Book Award from *Ploughshares.* He is the author of three other books of poetry, including *Black Maria* (2005) and *Jelly Roll* (2003), which was a finalist for both the National Book Award and the *Los Angeles Times* Book Prize and won the Paterson Poetry Prize. Young is also the editor of *Giant Steps: The New Generation of African American Writers* (2000). Young is currently Atticus Haygood Professor of English and Creative Writing and curator of the Danowski Poetry Collection at Emory University.

Acknowledgments

"When" © 2005 by Elizabeth Alexander, reprinted from *American Sublime* with the permission of Graywolf Press, St. Paul, Minnesota. **"seven crown man"** (Holly Bass) first appeared in *nocturnes 3: (re)view of the literary arts.* **"Blessing the Lepers"** (Gloria Burgess) was originally a public-action performance as part of *Community*, which debuted at Third Place Commons in Seattle, Washington, during the 2005 tribute to Dr. Martin Luther King, Jr. It is also included in *The Open Door* (Read Oak Press, 2001). **"[surely i am able to write poems]"** (Lucille Clifton), from *Mercy.* Copyright © 2004 by Lucille Clifton. Reprinted with the permission of BOA Editions, Ltd., www.BDAEditions.org. **"Search for Robert Hayden"** © 2004 by Kyle Dargan, reprinted from *The Listening* with the permission of University of Georgia Press. **"Atlantic Coasts"** (Jarita Davis) first appeared in the *Crab Orchard Review.* **"Goodbye Porkpie Hat"** (Michael Harper) appeared in *nocturne 3: (re)view of the literary arts*, and in *Use Trouble*, (University of Illinois Press, 2005). *Our Book on Trane, The Yaddo Sessions*, by Paul Austerlitz, bass clarinet, and Michael S. Harper, vocals, appeared in 2004 cd format; two Brown University colleagues "on the road," in a studio outside of Saratoga Springs, New York, just before "The Travers": "all artists are here to disturb the peace." © Michael S. Harper. **"Phøu"** © 2003 by Duriel E. Harris, reprinted from *Drag* with the permission of Elixir Press. **"MT in Solitary"**(Reggie Harris) first appeared in the *African American Review.* **"Nigger Street 1937"** (Sean Hill) first appeared in *Pleiades.* **"Family Outing"** (Linda Susan Jackson) first appeared in *Rivendell.* **"Muse, a Lady Cautioning"** © 2003 by Honorée Fanonne Jeffers, reprinted from *Outlandish Blues* with the permission of Wesleyan University Press. **"Kind of Blue"** (A. Van Jordan) was previously published in *Rise* (Tia Chucha Press). **"The Haymarket"** (John Keene) first appeared in *SOLO Magazine* and won the SOLO Press Poetry Prize. **"long way home"**© by Quraysh Ali Lansana, reprinted from *They Shall Run: Harriet Tubman Poems* with the permission of Third World Press. **"Understanding Al Green"** © 2003 by Adrian Matejka, reprinted from *The Devil's Garden* with the permission of Alice James Books. **"An Offering"** © 2003 by Shara McCallum, reprinted from *Song of Thieves* with the permission of the University of Pittsburgh Press. **"A Quiet Rhythm of Sleep"** (Lenard D. Moore) first appeared in *Obsidian III.* **"Drinking Mojitos in Cuba Libra"** author Harryette Mullen wishes to thank the following journals and editors: *Callaloo*, Charles Rowell; *Volt*, Cal Bedient and Gillian Conoley; and *X-tra*, Allan deSouza. **"The Poet, 1955"** (Kevin Simmonds) first appeared in *Rhino.* **"Duende"** (Tracy K. Smith) first appeared in *Gulf Coast.* **"Dress"** © 2005 by Amber Flora Thomas, reprinted from *Eye of Water* with the permission of the University of Pittsburgh Press. Amber Flora Thomas's "Dress," winner of the 2001 Ann Stanford Poetry Prize, first appeared in volume

18 of the *Southern California Anthology*. **"Book of Ruth"** (Carolyn Beard Whitlow) first appeared in the *Kenyon Review*. **"Hard Headed Blues"** (Kevin Young) first appeared in the *Virginia Quarterly Review*. Reprinted by permission of the author, © Kevin Young, 2003.

Text design by Mary H. Sexton

Typesetting by Huron Valley Graphics, Ann Arbor, Michigan

Font is Janson Text
Designed by the Hungarian Nicholas Kis in about 1690,
the model for Janson Text was mistakenly attributed to the
Dutch printer Anton Janson. Kis' original matrices were found
in Germany and acquired by the Stempel foundry in 1919.
Its strong design and clear stroke contrast combine to create
text that is both elegant and easy to read.

        —Courtesy www.adobe.com

DATE DUE			
GAYLORD	No. 2333		PRINTED IN U.S.A.